Volume **6** **THE GOLDEN BOOK ENCYCLOPEDIA**

eagle to eye

An exciting, up-to-date encyclopedia
in 20 fact-filled, entertaining volumes

Especially designed as
a first encyclopedia for
today's grade-school children

More than 2,500 full-color
photographs and illustrations

From the Publishers of Golden® Books

Western Publishing Company, Inc.
Racine, Wisconsin 53404

ILLUSTRATION CREDITS
(t=top, b=bottom, c=center, l=left, r=right)

1 lf, John Rice/Joseph, Mindlin & Mulvey; 4, Robert Frank/Artist Network; 5 tl, Bettmann Archive; 5 cr, David Lindroth Inc.; 6 tr, NASA; 6 tl, David Lindroth Inc.; 8, Tom Powers/Joseph, Mindlin & Mulvey; 9 bl, J. Fennell/Bruce Coleman Inc.; 9 br, E.R. Degginger/Bruce Coleman Inc.; 10–11, Fiona Reid/Artist Network; 12–13 b, U.S. Geological Survey; 13 inset, Tom Powers/Joseph, Mindlin & Mulvey; 14, Tom McHugh/Photo Researchers; 15 br, Mei-Ku Huang, M.D./Evelyne Johnson Associates; 16, Royal Worcester Spode USA; 17 tl, Tony Howarth/Woodfin Camp; 17 br, Frank Mayo; 18 tl and cl, Tom Powers/Joseph, Mindlin & Mulvey; 18 tr, NASA; 19, J.C. Carton/Bruce Coleman Inc.; 20–21 b, Rebecca Merrilees/Joseph, Mindlin & Mulvey; 21 tl, Joy Spurr/Bruce Coleman Inc.; 22, Steve Solum/Bruce Coleman Inc.; 23 br, Marilyn Bass; 23 t, Michael O'Reilly/Joseph, Mindlin & Mulvey; 24 t, Tom Myers/Photo Researchers; 24 cl, Susan Goldstein; 25, Gary Lippincott/Publisher's Graphics; 26 bl, Valerie Taylor/Bruce Coleman Inc.; 26 br, E.R. Degginger/Bruce Coleman Inc.; 27 tl, Jeff Foott/Bruce Coleman Inc.; 27 br, John Rice/Joseph, Mindlin & Mulvey; 28 cr, Marc Bernheim/Woodfin Camp; 29 and 30 t, Jim Pickerell; 30 inset, M. Timothy O'Keefe/Bruce Coleman Inc.; 31, Borromeo/EPA/Art Resource; 32 bl, Bettmann Archive; 32 br, Marilyn Bass; 33, U.S. Navy & Dwight D. Eisenhower Library; 34 and 35, Gary Lippincott/Publisher's Graphics; 37 t, Ontario Science Centre, Toronto; 37 inset, Barry Parker/Bruce Coleman Inc.; 38 tl, Brad Hamann; 38 br, Michael O'Reilly/Joseph, Mindlin & Mulvey; 39 tl, Richard Hutchings/Photo Researchers; 39 r, Rollison/Sygma; 39 cl and 40 both, Brad Hamann; 41, Lee Foster/Bruce Coleman Inc.; 42–43 and 43 br, Tom Powers/Joseph, Mindlin & Mulvey; 44, Ferranti Electronics/A. Sternberg/S.P.L./Photo Researchers; 45 t, Brad Hamann; 45 b and 46 bl, Sandy Rabinowitz/Publisher's Graphics; 46 br, NASA; 47, Bob Gossington/Bruce Coleman Inc.; 51, Lloyd P. Birmingham; 52, The Photo Source; 53, UPI/Bettmann Newsphotos; 54 b, Sarkis Buckaklian; 54 inset, used by permission of the publisher from *The Baseball Encyclopedia*, Seventh Edition, Joseph L. Reichler, Editor. Copyright ©1988 Macmillan Publishing Company, a division of Macmillan, Inc.; 55, Marilyn Bass; 56 and 57, Juan Barberis/Artist Network; 58, Bettmann Archive; 59 both, Brad Hamann; 60 c, Historical Pictures Service, Chicago; 61 both, Brad Hamann; 62 and 63 br, Tim Graham/Sygma; 64 tr, Historical Pictures Service, Chicago; 64 bl, Scala/Art Resource; 65, David Lindroth Inc.; 66 and 67, Marilyn Bass; 70, Régis Bossu/Sygma; 71 tl, Reynolds Aluminum; 71 bl, Jeffrey D. Smith/Woodfin Camp; 72, David Lindroth Inc.; 73 bl, © Joe Viesti; 73 br, David Lindroth Inc.; 74 and 75 tl, © Joe Viesti; 75 br and 76 tl, William Bacon/Photo Researchers; 77 bl, Thomas Hopker/Woodfin Camp; 78 cr, © Joe Viesti; 78–79 t, Norwegian Tourist Board; 79 tr, David Lindroth Inc.; 79 cl, Alon Reininger/Woodfin Camp; 81 bl, Arthur Sirdofsky; 81 t, David Lindroth Inc.; 82 both, Adam Woolfitt/Woodfin Camp; 83, Haeseler Art Publishers/Art Resource; 84, David Lindroth Inc.; 85 tl, G.D. Plage/Bruce Coleman Inc.; 85 b, Van Bucher/Photo Researchers; 86, John Shaw/Bruce Coleman Inc.; 87, Rebecca Merrilees/Joseph, Mindlin & Mulvey; 88, Fiona Reid/Artist Network; 89, Focus on Sports; 90 tl and tr, M.W.F. Tweedie/Bruce Coleman Inc.; 91, Bruce Lemerise/Joseph, Mindlin & Mulvey; 91 tr, Bettmann Archive; 92 tr, photo courtesy of The Cousteau Society, a member- supported non-profit environmental organization; 93, David Lindroth Inc.; 95 both, AP/Wide World; 96 tr, J.O. Grande/Bruce Coleman Inc.; 96 bl and br, Robert Frank/Artist Network.

COVER CREDITS
Center: Steve Solum/Bruce Coleman Inc. Clockwise from top: Western Publishing Company, Inc.; Jim Pickerell; J.O. Grande/Bruce Coleman Inc.; Brad Hamann; Scala/Art Resource; Jeff Foott/Bruce Coleman Inc.

Library of Congress Catalog Card Number: 87-82741
ISBN: 0-307-70106-9

ABCDEFGHIJK

The letter *E* was written this way by ancient tribes in the Middle East. They used it for the *h* sound.

The ancient Greeks called it *epsilon*, and used it first for the *he* sound, then for the *e* sound only.

When the ancient Romans borrowed it, they turned it around. It looked just like our capital *E*.

eagle

The eagle is a large, powerful bird. It has strong wings, a hooked beak, and long, sharp claws. It hunts for food in the daytime, using its excellent eyesight to spot its prey. When the eagle sees a small animal, it swoops down and picks up the animal in its

Three eagles, including the bald eagle, a symbol of the United States.

harpy eagle

bald eagle

golden eagle

claws. Then it flies to a tall tree or other high place. There, it uses its beak to tear the food into small pieces.

Some eagles hunt in open country. Their long wings enable them to glide and soar on currents of rising air. Eagles that live in forests usually have shorter wings. This makes it easier to fly between trees. They do not soar.

Eagles are valuable birds. They eat rodents and other pests. They also *scavenge*—look for the meat of dead animals.

Eagles build their nests high in trees or on rocky cliffs. The nests, called *aeries,* are made of sticks and lined with leaves and grass. Many eagles use the same nests year after year. They repair and add to their nests each year, until the nests become very large. One nest in Ohio was used for 36 years. It weighed almost a ton!

A female eagle lays one or two eggs. When the babies hatch, they are helpless. Both parents take care of the babies, called *eaglets.* They feed the eaglets and later teach them how to fly.

There are many kinds of eagles. Some kinds have feathers on their legs. They are called booted eagles because their leg feathers may look like boots. Fish eagles live near water and feed mostly on fish. One of the best-known fish eagles is the bald eagle. It lives in North America—and it is not bald. It may have gotten this name because it has white feathers on its head. Its body and wings are dark brown. The golden eagle, known as the "king of birds," has yellow-tipped feathers on its head and neck.

Harpy eagles may be more than a meter (3 feet) long. Their feet are as large as people's hands! Harpy eagles live in rain forests in Central and South America, where they hunt monkeys and sloths. Snake eagles are found mainly in Africa and Asia. They eat snakes and other reptiles. Their toes have thick soles and their legs are protected by scales.

People think of eagles as symbols of strength, courage, and freedom. For this reason, people have long used eagles on flags, coins, and national seals. The bald eagle is the national symbol of the United States. In the United States, bald eagles and golden eagles are protected by law.

See also **birds of prey** and **bird.**

ear

The ear makes it possible to hear sound. All sounds begin when something starts to *vibrate*—move back and forth very quickly. This causes air to move in waves. Your external ear—outer ear—is shaped like a shell to collect some of these sound waves. (*See* **sound.**)

The real working part of the ear is the internal ear. It is divided into two parts—the middle ear and inner ear. The first part of the middle ear is called the *eardrum.* As sound waves hit your eardrum, it begins to move back and forth. It pushes against three tiny bones, called the *hammer,* the *anvil,* and the *stirrup.* The bones push against a membrane that runs down the center of a coiled tube. This tube is located in your inner ear, and it is filled with liquid. The membrane is covered with tiny hairs—250,000 of them! The pumping movement of the bones starts the membrane moving. When the membrane moves, the liquid pushes against the tiny hairs. The hairs are connected to nerves that send messages to your brain. When the messages reach your brain, they are interpreted as sounds.

Your ear helps you keep your balance. Three other canals in the ear are filled with liquid and lined with hairs. Whenever your head moves, the liquid moves. This causes the hairs inside the canals to move, sending messages to the brain that make you aware of how you are moving.

See also **hearing.**

The ear collects sound waves and changes them into signals that the auditory nerve can send to the brain. The ear also gives us our sense of balance.

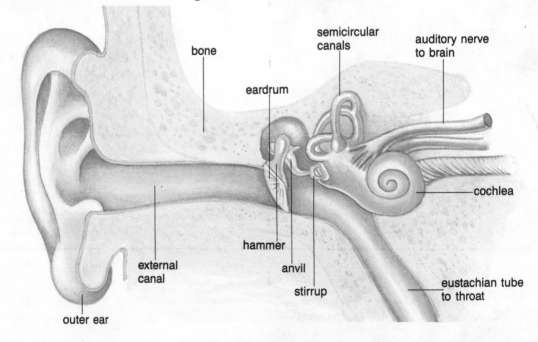

Amelia Earhart was the first woman to fly across the Atlantic Ocean alone.

Earhart, Amelia

Amelia Earhart was an American flier in the early days of aviation. She was the first woman to fly across the Atlantic, and the first woman to fly across it alone. She was also the first woman to receive the Distinguished Flying Cross.

Amelia Earhart was born in Atchison, Kansas, in 1897. As a youngster, she loved to explore nearby caves. She built a "roller coaster" in her backyard. When she took her first ride in a rickety little plane in 1920, she knew she wanted to become a flier.

To earn money for lessons, she took a job as a telephone operator. Within a year, she had her pilot's license. But there was no way for her to earn a living as a pilot. She tried social work and teaching. Still, her dreams centered on flying.

In 1928, she became the first woman to cross the Atlantic as a passenger in an airplane. In 1932, she flew across alone and became world-famous.

In 1937, Amelia set out to fly around the world by the longest route—along the equator. She and her navigator completed more than half the flight. Then they vanished, over the Pacific Ocean. What happened to them remains a mystery.

Earth

Earth is our home. We have lived on Earth all of our lives. Yet we do not know everything about our planet.

Earth and Its Neighbors Photographs of Earth taken from space show a blue-and-white ball surrounded by black emptiness. From such pictures, you might not guess that Earth is part of a family, but it is. Earth belongs to a family of four planets. They are called the *terrestrial* planets, from the Latin word *terra,* meaning "earth." The three other family members—Venus, Mercury, and Mars—are like Earth in some ways. They, too, are made of rock and iron and are small compared with such planets as Jupiter and Saturn.

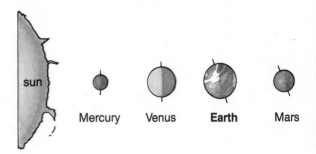

sun   Mercury   Venus   **Earth**   Mars

Earth is the third-closest planet to the sun. Mercury and Venus are closer.

Although it is small compared to the sun and some other planets, Earth is still very large. Earth's diameter is almost 13,000 kilometers (almost 8,000 miles). Its circumference is almost 40,000 kilometers (25,000 miles). Earth is so large that even the highest mountains are like bumps on an orange compared to its total surface.

Moving Through Space The Earth does not stand still in space. It spins like a top on its *axis*—an imaginary line between the North Pole and the South Pole. It also travels in a nearly circular path around the sun.

It takes Earth 24 hours to make one complete turn on its axis. As it turns, half of Earth faces the sun while the other half faces away. This is why periods of darkness

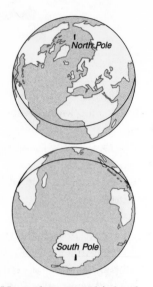

More than two-thirds of Earth's surface is water (above). Right, from space, Earth looks like a "big blue marble."

(night) follow periods of daylight in regular order. One 24-hour day is made up of one period of daylight plus one of darkness.

If you wanted to travel around Earth in one day along the equator, you would have to whiz along at a speed of more than 1,600 kilometers (1,000 miles) per hour. This is how fast any point on the equator is moving at any time of day or night. Closer to the poles, the speed of rotation is slower. At either the North Pole or the South Pole, the speed of rotation is zero. If you stood at one of the poles, you would still turn around once every 24 hours, but you would not actually travel any distance.

Since Earth spins so fast on its axis, you may wonder why we are not all flung off into space. The force that prevents this from happening is called *gravity*. Gravity not only keeps us on Earth, it also keeps our planet's only natural satellite, the moon, circling around Earth. (*See* **gravity** and **moon**.)

Earth is not quite perfectly round. The spinning causes a bulge around the equator, so Earth·is slightly fatter around its "waist." But its circumference around the equator is only about 80 kilometers (50 miles) greater than its circumference measured around the poles. Also, Earth's northern half is slightly larger than its southern half.

Earth's path around the sun is called its *orbit*. Traveling at a speed of 106,000 kilometers (66,000 miles) per hour, it takes Earth about 365¼ days—one year—to make a complete trip around the sun. Earth covers a distance of almost 940 million kilometers (over 580 million miles) each time it makes this annual trip.

The Outer Earth The surface of the earth measures over 510 million square kilometers (almost 200 million square miles). About seven-tenths of this surface is covered by water. This water consists of the four great oceans—the Pacific, Atlantic, Indian, and Arctic—as well as all the bays, lakes, streams, and rivers. The remaining three-tenths of Earth's surface is land, mostly divided into seven great landmasses called *continents*. Above the surface of the earth stretches an envelope of air called the *atmosphere*. It is more than 1,100 kilometers (700 miles) high. (*See* **continent; ocean;** and **atmosphere.**)

Below the surface, Earth is divided into three zones: crust, mantle, and core.

The *crust* is Earth's thin outer "skin." It is mostly solid rock, although it includes the soil and sand as well. Along with air, water, and sunlight, the crust provides animals and plants with everything they need to live and

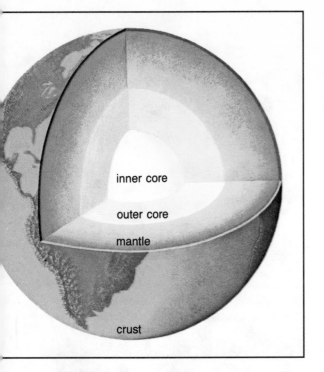

inner core

outer core

mantle

crust

People have seen only Earth's thin crust, which is made of solid rock. Scientists believe that the mantle and the core are made of rock or metals so hot that they are liquid.

grow. The rocks of the crust provide the soil with minerals that plants depend on.

The crust is made of two main kinds of rock. The rocks of the continents tend to be lighter in color and not as heavy as the rocks of the ocean floor. The crust may be only 5 kilometers (3 miles) thick beneath the oceans. It can be 70 kilometers (40 miles) thick where there are high mountains on the continents.

Earth's crust is a very active zone. We can sometimes see or feel this activity—for example, when a volcano erupts. But most of the activity is so slow that we are unaware of it. The crust is broken in many places, and the broken parts can move against each other. Usually, the movement is slow and smooth, so we do not know it is happening. But once in a while, part of the crust will give a sudden lurch that we can see and feel even if we live 200 kilometers (120 miles) away. That kind of movement is called an *earthquake*. (*See* **earthquake**.)

The Inner Earth The zone beneath the crust is called the *mantle*. The mantle is about 2,900 kilometers (1,800 miles) thick. It is much hotter than the crust. The mantle is made of rock so hot that it can flow like a thick liquid. Sometimes, the mantle oozes up from cracks in the crust under the oceans. It pours out on the floor of the ocean, forming new crust. (*See* **continental drift**.)

Below the mantle lies the third and last of Earth's zones—the *core*. Scientists think Earth's core consists mostly of iron and nickel. The inner core and the outer core together are about 3,500 kilometers (2,200 miles) thick. Even the deepest holes we drill cannot reach it, so we must learn about the core without actually seeing it. Records of earthquake waves that have passed through Earth have given us important information. These waves show that the outer core is liquid, while the inner core is solid. We also know that the core is not a perfectly smooth ball. It has bumps and pits that can change the speed of Earth's rotation slightly. The heat and pressure within the core are greater by far than anywhere else on Earth. The temperature can be as high as 5,000° C (9,000° F).

Changes on Earth Earth is almost 150 million kilometers (93 million miles) away from the sun. This distance keeps temperatures on most places on Earth just right for life—not too hot and not too cold. Of course, temperatures change as the seasons change, but plants and animals have evolved in such a way that they can adjust to these changes. (*See* **evolution**.)

Why does Earth have seasonal changes of temperature and weather? The reason is that Earth does not sit up perfectly straight as it spins. It is tilted at an angle of 23½°. This means that as Earth spins, the North Pole sometimes points in one direction and sometimes points in another. For example, on June 21, the day that summer begins in the northern half of Earth, the North Pole leans toward the sun. On December 22, the day that winter begins, the North Pole leans away from the sun.

See also **earth history** and **solar system**.

earth history

Scientists did not begin studying the history of our planet until the late 1700s. At that time, geologists in Scotland and England began asking themselves how the earth formed and how old it was.

These geologists recognized that some rocks are formed from *sediment*—dust, mud, and sand. They knew how slowly sediment builds up and turns into rock. So they decided that it must have taken millions of years—not thousands—for the rocks to form. But the geologists had no way of telling how many millions of years.

Then, at the beginning of the 1900s, scientists discovered how to use the natural radioactivity of rocks as a kind of clock. They were able to tell how much time had passed since the rocks were formed. To their surprise, geologists found that the earth was much older than they had suspected. Instead of being millions of years old, the earth was between 4 and 5 *billion* years old! (*See* **geology; dates and dating;** and **radioactivity.**)

From a Gas Cloud to Oceans Scientists think that about 5 billion years ago, there was an enormous cloud of gas and dust where our solar system is today. Part of that cloud became the sun, and part became the planets. The cloud began to draw together because of gravity. (*See* **gravity.**)

The cloud particles that became the earth grew hotter as they drew together. The heat may have been caused by increasing pressure, or the new earth may have been heated by large objects falling into it. The earth became so hot that it melted. Gravity drew the heaviest elements toward the earth's center. The lighter elements formed a crust on the earth's surface. (*See* **Earth.**)

Gases released by erupting volcanoes formed the first atmosphere. Water vapor from the volcanoes formed clouds. The vapor could not form oceans, because the crust was too hot for water to collect on it. Its temperature was over 100° C (212° F), the boiling point of water.

Scientists believe that the solar system—the sun and the planets— grew from a giant cloud of gas (above).

As the crust became thicker, it blocked the heat from the hot rock beneath it. The surface of the earth began to cool. By about 4 billion years ago, the surface was cool enough for water to remain on it without boiling away. The first seas began to appear.

The Beginnings of Life Life began to develop in these ancient seas. The earliest forms of life on our planet were algae and bacteria. The algae were primitive one-celled plants. Some of them lived in large groups at depths of 10 meters (30 feet) or more. (*See* **algae** and **bacteria.**)

Some early forms of life probably got their energy from chemicals in the oceans. But the early algae were able to obtain their energy from sunlight. Sunlight helped the algae unlock the oxygen held in water and carbon dioxide molecules. The released oxygen had an important effect on the next 3½ billion years of the earth's history. (*See* **photosynthesis.**)

The Changing Atmosphere As algae produced oxygen, this gas accumulated in the atmosphere and oceans. It was probably poisonous to life forms that lived on chemicals. The newly released oxygen reacted with other elements in the crust. Iron rusted for the first time and caused great beds of red rock to appear.

Before there was much oxygen, the atmosphere could not block the sun's ultraviolet rays. The rays made the land and the surface of the sea unsafe for life. When there was enough oxygen in the atmosphere to filter ultraviolet rays, the top layer of ocean water became safe for life. New forms of plant and animal life were able to come into being. (*See* **ultraviolet light.**)

At the same time that oxygen was becoming plentiful in the atmosphere, carbon dioxide was building up in the oceans. Sea creatures used it to develop shells for protection. Other creatures began to develop skeletons to support their bodies.

Beginning of the Fossil Record We learn the story of life on Earth partly by looking at *fossils*—the remains that early living things left behind. Fossils teach us about the living things themselves, and also about what the Earth was like when these creatures were alive. Fossils of shells found on mountaintops tell us that these mountains were once part of the seafloor. Fossils show that Antarctica once had a mild climate, and that some deserts were once covered with water. (*See* **fossil.**)

The oceans became home to shell-building creatures about 570 million years ago. We know this because rocks of this age contain fossils of animals that had shells and skeletons. Rocks older than this show only imprints left by soft-bodied creatures.

This point in time marks a milestone in the history of the earth. The 4 billion years before it are called the Precambrian era. We know little about the Precambrian era because there were so few fossils. We know much more about the 570 million years that followed it. We have divided these years into three eras: Paleozoic (meaning "ancient life"), Mesozoic ("middle life"), and Cenozoic ("recent life").

Moving Plates and Life By the time the Paleozoic era began, the earth's crust had split into a number of parts, called *plates*. The plates of the earth's crust have been slowly moving ever since they first formed. That is why the outlines and positions of the oceans and continents have been steadily changing. (*See* **continental drift.**)

About the time that the first fish appeared, 500 million years ago, the North American and northern European plates began drifting toward each other. As the watery gap between them closed, some plants adapted to life on dry land. Then, about 400 million years ago, the first air-breathing creatures —insects—appeared on dry land.

Fossils are signs of living things that have turned to rock. At left, an imprint left by an ancient seashell. Right, a beetle trapped in a piece of amber.

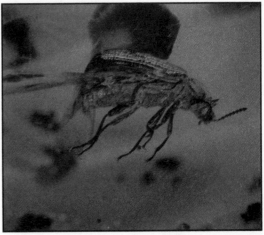

Scientists divide earth history into eras or ages.
Each age leaves particular kinds of rocks (below)
and the fossil remains of particular living things (above).
At first, all living things lived in seawater (left).
Later (right), some adapted to living on land.

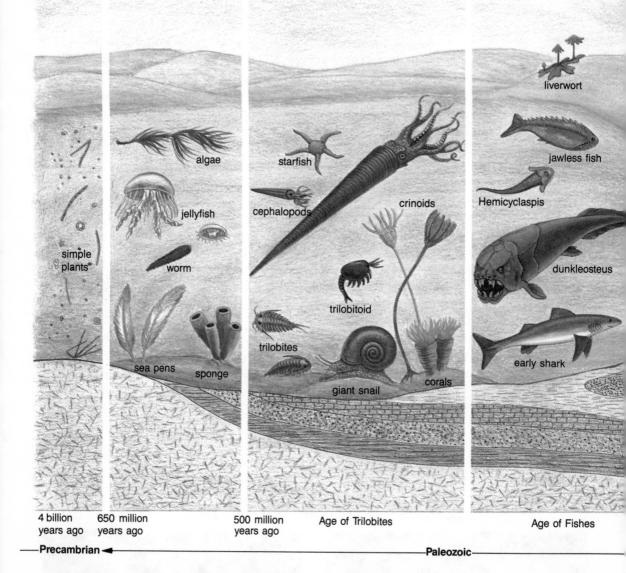

liverwort

algae

jawless fish

starfish

jellyfish

cephalopods

crinoids

Hemicyclaspis

simple plants

worm

dunkleosteus

trilobitoid

sea pens

sponge

trilobites

giant snail

corals

early shark

4 billion years ago

650 million years ago

500 million years ago

Age of Trilobites

Age of Fishes

—Precambrian ◄

Paleozoic

During the next 150 million years of the Paleozoic era, the seas between the continents were steadily closing up. During this period, amphibians—the first air-breathing creatures with backbones—made a home for themselves on dry land.

Much of the world's dry land was now clustered in the warm regions of the southern hemisphere. Great tropical forests of primitive trees and ferns grew in what today are North America and Europe. From the

fossil remains of these forests, huge deposits of coal would later form. (*See* **coal.**)

By the end of the Paleozoic era, all the continents had joined together in the southern hemisphere. As they collided with one another, sediment from the seafloor was caught between them and squeezed up. This crumpled sediment turned to rock and formed the roots of new mountain ranges, such as the Appalachians of North America. (*See* **mountain.**)

giant dragonfly
pterodactyl
Archaeopteryx
butterfly
gull
man
duck-billed dinosaur
conifer
magnolia
giant horsetail
stegosaur
giant club moss
mammoth
tyrannosaur
cockroach
Eohippus
horse
tree fern
scorpion
sabertooth
amphibian (Eryops)
brontosaur
glyptodon
sailback
elm
coelacanth
sunflower
ichthyosaur
dolphin
snake
plesiosaur

00 million years ago Age of Coal   250 million years ago   Age of Reptiles   65 million years ago Age of Mammals present

◄——————— Mesozoic ———————►◄——— Cenozoic ———►

Life in the Mesozoic Era By the time the Mesozoic era began, about 225 million years ago, reptiles had become the dominant form of life on land and in the water. One group of reptiles, the dinosaurs, were especially successful in adapting to new environments. (*See* **dinosaur** and **reptile.**)

During the Mesozoic era, the continents pulled apart from each other. Half of them formed one huge landmass in the northern hemisphere. The other half formed an equally large landmass in the southern hemisphere. Separating them was a great equatorial sea.

New forms of plant life evolved during the Mesozoic era. In the forests, cone-bearing trees began to grow, and later the first flowering plants appeared. About 200 million years ago, mammals came into being. About 50 million years later, they were followed by the first birds. (*See* **animals, prehistoric** and **birds of the past.**)

By the time the Mesozoic era ended, the huge landmass in the southern hemisphere—called Gondwanaland—had broken apart to form the five southern continents. The dinosaurs and other giant reptiles became extinct. North America tore away from Europe. To the west, the Rocky Mountains began to rise. (*See* **Rocky Mountains**.)

Recent Life The latest chapter of earth's history is the Cenozoic era, which began 65 million years ago. During this era, the world we are familiar with today took form. At the beginning of the era, the Alps of Europe began to rise. Europe and Africa squeezed shut the sea that had separated them. We now call what remains of this ancient sea the Mediterranean Sea. (*See* **Alps** and **Mediterranean Sea**.)

Later, India collided with Asia, crumpling and pushing up sedimentary rocks to form the world's highest mountains—the Himalayas. (*See* **Himalayas**.)

All the continents had nearly reached their present positions when the earth was overtaken by a period of intense cold. This period, called the Ice Age, lasted almost 2 million years. (*See* **ice age**.)

When the climate finally warmed up again, 10,000 years ago, the last woolly mammoth and saber-toothed cat had disappeared, and sea levels had risen. Modern man lived in a world of varied climates, where the rapid rise of civilization was possible.

earthquake

If you have ever felt the ground shake beneath your feet, you may have felt an earthquake. In some countries, a person may feel several earthquakes in a lifetime. In many places, earthquakes are very rare.

Small earthquakes may just rattle the dishes in a cabinet or knock a few pictures off the wall. Large earthquakes, however, are among the most dangerous of natural disasters. In 1556, an earthquake in China killed more than 830,000 people. More recently, in 1976, a major earthquake in China killed at least 240,000 people. The great San Franciso earthquake of 1906 killed fewer people—about 500. However, the city was almost completely destroyed. As recently as 1986, an earthquake in Mexico caused over 4,200 deaths.

The most active earthquake zone is along the Pacific Ocean (below). Earthquakes can split the earth (right)—usually along lines called *faults*.

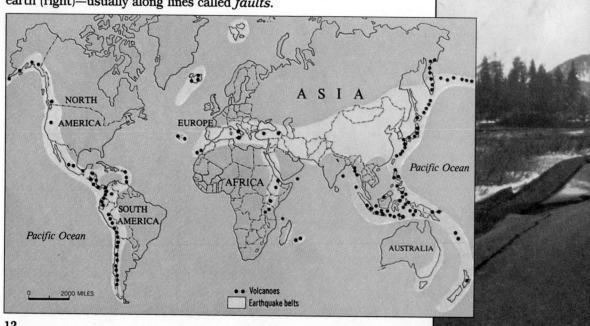

What Causes Earthquakes Earthquakes take place in Earth's *crust*—its thin outside layer. The crust is not a complete shell. It is broken up into about 20 huge rafts of rock called *plates*. Some plates are so large that an entire continent or ocean can fit on them. One large plate carries all of North America plus half the North Atlantic Ocean. Plates float on a layer of partly melted rock. Not all the plates are moving in the same direction. (*See* **continental drift.**)

The line where two plates meet is called a *fault*. The plate that supports the Pacific Ocean meets the North American plate along the San Andreas Fault. Along this fault, the two plates move side by side in opposite directions. Many earthquakes occur near the fault between plates. Large earthquakes occur where two plates are rubbing against each other, or where one plate is pushing under another.

The longest and deepest faults are where two plates meet. But faults can also exist within one plate. These faults are long, deep cracks that split the plate's crust into parts. Earthquakes happen when these parts shift. Earthquakes within a plate can be very

strong. The largest earthquake in United States history was in Missouri in 1811, deep in the North American plate. (*See* **geology.**)

Usually, the rock on either side of a fault moves slowly and steadily. But at some places along a fault, rocks on opposite sides of a fault get locked together. Movement stops in those places but continues elsewhere along the fault. The rocks where the fault is stuck are pulled, which causes them to stretch. The stretching may last for years, until the rocks cannot stretch any more. Then they snap, jumping back several feet at once.

When you stretch a rubber band, you are putting energy into it. The rubber band holds this energy until you let go. Then it snaps back, releasing the energy. Just like a rubber band, the rocks around the part of the fault that is stuck collect energy as they stretch. When they break, all that energy is suddenly let go. The more energy they have stored, the stronger the earthquake.

Earthquake Waves When this energy is released, it moves outward in waves, like the ripples from a stone dropped into a pool. These waves of energy, called *seismic waves*,

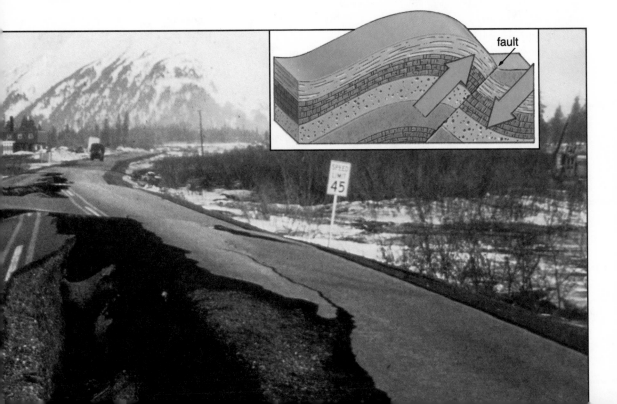

fault

travel through the earth at great speeds. They become weaker as they get farther away.

The seismic waves of an earthquake make the rocks they pass through vibrate. A strong earthquake releases so much energy that the vibrations can be felt and seen on the earth's surface. The ground may shake so violently that people are knocked down. When the shaking passes into the foundations of buildings and bridges, it may damage or destroy them. Fortunately, the shaking rarely lasts long.

Tsunamis Earthquakes can also happen under the sea. Sometimes the movement along an undersea fault raises or lowers great blocks of the ocean floor. This creates a special kind of water wave called a *tsunami.* As this wave approaches land, it grows higher and higher. By the time it reaches a shoreline, it may be a towering wall of water more than 12 meters (40 feet) high. Such waves can drown entire villages.

Similar waves can be caused by landslides into the water, or landslides that occur underwater. Most large landslides are also caused by earthquakes. The largest wave ever recorded was produced by a landslide caused by an earthquake. It was more than 500 meters (1,640 feet) high. Other tsunamis are caused by underwater volcanic explosions called *seaquakes.*

A moderately strong earthquake tumbled these freeway overpasses in California.

Predicting Earthquakes Scientists measure the strength of seismic waves with a *seismograph.* This instrument records the vibrations in the earth's surface. Depending on the strength of the vibrations it causes, an earthquake is given a number according to a system called the *Richter scale.* Large earthquakes measure 7 or more on the Richter scale. Seimologists study these records not only to measure earthquakes but to try to predict the time and place of future earthquakes. If they succeed, people can be evacuated before disaster strikes. This could save thousands of lives.

earthworm

Earthworms can be found almost anyplace that has soil and green plants. Earthworms live on farms and in city parks. They live in gardens and along the edges of roads.

Earthworms build burrows in the soil. They usually stay in their burrows during the day. If earthworms are put in the sun, their skin dries out and they die. When earthworms must come out during the day, they crawl under rocks, logs, or fallen leaves. There, they are hidden from the sun.

Most of the worms' feeding is done at night. Their favorite food is rotted plant matter. They also eat bits of living roots and leaves. An earthworm has a mouth but no teeth. Food is swallowed whole, then ground up in an organ called the *gizzard.* Earthworms also have no eyes, ears, or lungs.

There are many kinds of earthworms. Some are only .7 centimeter (1/4 inch) long, but others may be as long as 3 meters (11 feet). All have rings around their bodies. The rings divide the body into parts called *segments.* It is hard to tell which end of a worm is the head and which is the tail. The best way to tell is to watch a worm move. The head is the part that goes first. Also, the head is slightly pointed.

There are no male or female earthworms. Each earthworm has male and female organs. But two worms must mate in order to

Earthworms live underground in burrows. They come out at night to get food.

produce eggs. Earthworms lay their eggs in the soil. The eggs are in a case that protects them. The case looks like a small, yellowish pea. Each case contains several eggs. When the baby worms hatch, they look exactly like their parents. But the baby worms are much smaller—like tiny pieces of string.

Earthworms are very important. They help fertilize the soil by taking food down into it and carrying up their wastes. Their burrowing keeps soil loose and brings air and water into the soil. All of this keeps the soil in good condition, which helps plants grow.

Birds and many other animals eat earthworms. But people are the earthworms' worst enemies. Fishermen use worms as bait. Worms are also killed by insect-killing chemicals, plant-killing chemicals, and even heavy use of some fertilizers.

See also **worm.**

Easter

Easter is the most important Christian festival. It celebrates Jesus Christ's return to life after death on the cross. It also represents the idea of new life after death. Easter is the oldest Christian holiday.

Easter Sunday does not always fall on the same date each year. That is because Easter Sunday is on the Sunday after the first full moon of spring. In most Western countries, Easter Sunday occurs sometime between March 22 and April 25. The Eastern Orthodox church uses a different calendar, and so Orthodox Easter is often later than in Western churches.

Other religious dates depend on the date of Easter Sunday. The period of Lent includes the 40 days before Easter Sunday, not including Sundays. This is a time of repentance for sins. Holy Week is the last week before Easter Sunday. The period after Easter ends with Pentecost.

While Lent is a time of repenting and fasting, Easter Sunday is a joyous holiday. Churches are often decorated with white flowers and candles.

Many people wear new clothing at Easter. Some cities have Easter parades, in which people stroll along in their new clothes. Wearing new clothing is believed to come from the custom of baptizing new Christians in new white clothing at Easter.

The lamb is an important Easter symbol. The lamb represents Jesus Christ, the "Lamb of God." Eating lamb and desserts shaped like lambs is part of some traditional Easter celebrations.

Easter eggs are another part of Easter. People in many countries paint Easter eggs

These symbols of new life are often used in Easter celebrations.

with designs or pictures. There are also egg-rolling contests and egg-tapping contests to see who can keep an egg for the longest time without cracking it. Easter-egg hunts are another part of Easter fun. Eggs are believed to be symbols of new life. They played a part in customs that began before Christianity.

Rabbits and baby chicks are also symbols of spring and new life. In the United States, the Easter Bunny is supposed to bring Easter eggs and small gifts to children. Chocolate and candy bunnies and chicks are favorite Easter treats.

East Germany, *see* Germany

eating customs

All people need to eat. But people in different parts of the world eat very different foods. They eat at different times of the day and with different tools. They also behave differently when they eat. What people eat, when they eat, and how they eat are called their eating customs.

Meals In the United States, breakfast, lunch, and dinner are the usual meals. Breakfast is often eaten before going to work or school. Early American settlers who lived and worked on farms often ate large breakfasts. They did their chores for an hour or two before eating. That gave them big appetites. Today, most people eat smaller breakfasts. Cereal is considered a breakfast food. So are toast, eggs, and juice. In Europe, people may eat a roll and drink coffee or tea. In England, breakfast may include cooked fish and grilled tomatoes. In China, it may be rice soup.

Lunch is eaten around noon in the United States. Sandwiches, soup, and salads are popular lunch foods for people in school or at work.

In the United States, dinner or supper is often the largest meal. In many homes, it is the one meal families eat together.

Each guest at this formal dinner has many plates, glasses, and eating utensils.

In other countries around the world, the eating pattern is different. In many Spanish-speaking countries, lunch is much later in the day—after two or three o'clock. Dinner may not be until nine or ten in the evening. In England, people have a snack called *elevenses* between breakfast and lunch. They may also have an afternoon snack called *tea.* Many offices and factories in the United States have coffee breaks at midmorning and midafternoon.

Eating Tools In the United States and many other countries, tables are set with forks, knives, spoons, plates, and glasses. Knives are the oldest eating tools. Spoons came next. Forks came much later. In fact, when forks were first introduced to England, they were considered foolish. People were expected to eat with fingers or knives.

In China and Japan, people eat with a pair of slim, straight sticks called *chopsticks.* It is considered bad manners to use a knife while eating. Food is often cut up into bite-size pieces before it is cooked.

In many parts of the world, people eat with their fingers. Everyone may help themselves from one big bowl or pot. Sometimes, there

These desert people eat from one big plate. They must eat only with their right hands.

is no table. Instead, a cloth is spread on the floor.

Table Manners Good manners are what the people of a particular place consider to be good manners. In most of Europe and America, it is bad manners to burp while eating. In some places in Asia and Africa, a person is supposed to burp after eating. The burp means that the person has eaten enough and is satisfied.

In some parts of Europe, keeping both hands on the table is not good manners. Yet in some parts of America, it is good manners to keep both hands above the table. In Muslim countries, food must be eaten with the right hand.

Even within one country, eating customs vary with the location. In a fancy restaurant, people are expected to act differently from the way they act on a picnic or in a fast-food restaurant.

If you are in a new place, it is a good idea to watch others. In the United States, it is bad manners to eat with your fingers in a good restaurant. But it is bad manners to demand a fork and knife in a country where people do eat with their fingers.

echo

Have you ever called out in an empty room and heard your own voice repeating itself a split second later? What you heard was an echo. It was caused by sound reflecting —bouncing back—from a surface, like a rubber ball.

To cause an echo, two things are necessary. First, there must be a wall or other hard, flat surface from which the sound waves can bounce. Second, you must be standing at least 10 meters (30 feet) from that surface. The sound waves carrying your voice will travel to the wall, bounce off, and then return to your ear. If you are standing closer to the wall, the sound waves will bounce back too fast for you to hear the echo separately.

Sound travels about 330 meters (1,100 feet) a second in air. If you stand 33 meters (110 feet) from a large wall and call loudly, the sound will take one-tenth of a second to reach the wall. Your echo will bounce back to your ears in another one-tenth of a second. The farther away you stand, the longer it takes to hear the echo. This way of finding out how far away objects are is called *echolocation*. Bats find their way by echolocation. People used this idea to develop sonar—a way of finding objects underwater by using sound waves. (*See* **bat** and **radar and sonar**.)

See also **sound**.

Sound echoes— bounces—off a mountain and back to the sound maker.

SOLAR ECLIPSE

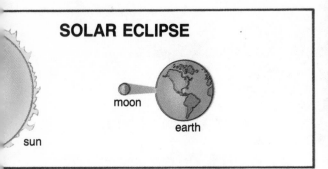

In a solar eclipse (above and right), the sun's light is blocked out on a small region of Earth by the moon's shadow. In a lunar eclipse (below), Earth gets between the sun and the moon so that the moon cannot reflect any light from the sun.

LUNAR ECLIPSE

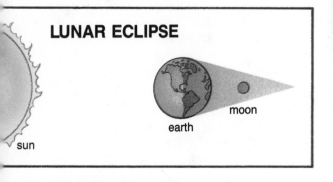

eclipse

We see an eclipse here on earth as a sudden and strange darkening of the sun or moon for a short time. In ancient times, people were frightened by eclipses and believed they were warnings of future misfortune. People made up stories about sky dragons eating the sun, and similar tales. Today, we know why eclipses happen. Out in space, the moon and the earth sometimes pass between one another and the sun. The sun or moon seems to darken because the sun's light is temporarily blocked out during the eclipse.

Solar Eclipses A solar eclipse is the most dramatic eclipse we see here on Earth. Everyone has seen what happens when a thick cloud passes in front of the sun. Suddenly, it gets much darker outside, even though it is the middle of the day. It gets darker during a

solar eclipse, too, only more so. Instead of a cloud blocking the sun, we see what appears to be a shadowy black disk moving directly in front of the sun.

That black disk is really the moon. It is the cause of a solar eclipse. As the moon orbits around the earth, it sometimes passes directly between the sun and the earth. When this happens, we have a solar eclipse on Earth. If the moon is lined up so that it completely blocks out the sun, the eclipse is called *total.* If the moon blocks out only part of the sun, the eclipse is called *partial.*

You may wonder how the moon could ever completely block out the sun. After all, the sun is 400 times larger than the moon. But when we see them in the sky, the sun and moon look about the same size. How can that be? The moon, just by chance, is also 400 times closer to the earth than the sun is. A close, small object may look bigger than a large, faraway object. For example, if you hold your hand in front of your eyes, it can completely cover a car that is a block away from you. Try it, and you will understand how the moon can block out the sun during an eclipse.

You can learn something else about a solar eclipse with this experiment. Put your hand up again so that you block out the same car. Now, keep your hand in the same position, but move your head slightly. You will not have to move your head very far before the car comes into view. But you, your hand, and the car all have to be in a straight line in order for this experiment to work.

The same kind of straight line is needed for a solar eclipse. When a solar eclipse is happening, there is only a small part of the world where it can be seen. That area has the correct positions of sun (the car), moon (your hand), and viewing position (you). People along the path of the eclipse will see the sky darken and the moon cross in front of the sun. The path is only 300 kilometers (186 miles) wide. Outside that area, the sun will shine as always.

A total solar eclipse occurs somewhere on Earth about every year and a half. But the path of each eclipse covers only a small part of Earth. As a result, the average time between total solar eclipses in any one place is 300 years.

Caution: Never look at the sun, even during a solar eclipse. If you want to see the eclipse, ask a teacher or parent to explain how you can see it safely.

Lunar Eclipses In a lunar eclipse, the sun, moon, and earth are again lined up, but in a different way. This time, the earth is lined up *between* the sun and moon.

Usually, we see the moon as a brightly shining object in the night sky. But the moon does not give off light the way the sun does. It just reflects the sun's light.

What happens in a lunar eclipse is that the moon moves directly behind the earth. That puts the earth right between the moon and sun. Earth then blocks off sunlight going to the moon. As the moon moves in behind the earth, it grows very dim. You can still see it, because some light reaches it from sunlight spread out by Earth's atmosphere. But that filtered light gives the eclipsed moon a reddish-brown color.

Lunar eclipses are much more frequent than solar eclipses. There may be 20 lunar eclipses in 18 years over one area on Earth. Unlike solar eclipses, lunar eclipses can be seen wherever the moon is visible at the time of eclipse. Also, a total lunar eclipse can last more than an hour, compared to a few minutes for a solar eclipse.

Other Eclipses Solar and lunar eclipses are the two best known eclipses, but they are not the only ones. Other planets in our solar system regularly block our view of certain distant stars, and stars sometimes block our view of other stars. These are all eclipses, too.

Such eclipses have been very important in astronomy. For example, when a planet blocks a distant star, the time of the eclipse can be measured very accurately. This information can then be used to figure out the exact size of the planet.

See also **solar system; sun; moon;** and **astronomy.**

---

ecology

The earth is made up of living things and things that are not alive. Ecology is the study of how living things live in their surroundings—their *environment*. It is also concerned with the ways living things and nonliving things affect one another.

When an oxpecker eats insects off this Cape buffalo, both animals benefit.

Here is a short story of the life of a familiar bird, the American robin. Robins make nests in trees. They dig worms for food. Each spring, they lay several light blue eggs. When the eggs hatch, the parents feed the young robins. Soon the youngsters can fly. They now feed on their own. When autumn comes, the robins fly south, where it is warmer. They dig for worms in a new place. In spring, the robins fly north to begin the cycle again.

Every living thing needs certain things to stay alive. All living things must have food, water and a place to live and grow. Plants send down roots into the soil for nutrients and water, and to anchor them to a place to live. Bacteria and protists are tiny one-celled living things. They must have a damp place to live, or they dry up and die. Animals move around. They must have shelter for protection and a place to have their young.

Habitats   The place where a living thing gets what it needs to live is called its *habitat*. Different living things have different habitats. A polar bear lives in a cold habitat. A cactus lives in a hot, dry habitat. A fish lives in a watery habitat. A horseshoe crab lives in a seashore habitat.

Each habitat has different living things in it. A hardwood forest is the habitat of many living things, including trees, flowers, squirrels, rabbits, and chickadees. A grassland is another habitat. Prairie dogs, kingsnakes, mice, and grasses live in grasslands.

There are many water habitats, such as lakes, rivers, and oceans. Living things in lakes and rivers live in freshwater. Living things in oceans live in saltwater. Freshwater and saltwater habitats are different.

Many fish live in lakes. Frogs and turtles live in lakes, too. Insects live in and around lakes. They are food for frogs and many fish.

Many insects live on and under the rocks in rivers. Some fish, like trout, can live in rivers that move fast. But most fish live in parts of a river where the water moves slowly.

Hundreds of kinds of fish live in the oceans. Most ocean animals live near the shore. Seals feed in the ocean, but sleep and sun themselves on the shore. One-celled living things called *diatoms* float near the surface of the ocean. Many animals—even huge whales—eat these tiny living things.

Living Things in a Community   The things that live together in a habitat are called a *community*. They depend on one another. One way they depend on one another is for food. In a grassland community, grasses make their own food. Mice and prairie dogs eat the grasses. Snakes eat the mice and prairie dogs.

Living things depend on each other in other ways, too. Trees are homes for many animals. Birds and squirrels make nests on their branches. Mice and moles dig burrows around the bases of trees. Insects live under the bark of trees. Worms, insects, and other small animals make homes among the leaves that fall on the ground. Fungi grow on and under the leaves.

Sometimes, different living things become partners. This relationship is called *symbiosis*. Fungi and algae live together in a lichen. The algae make food. The fungi cover the algae and keep them from drying out. In Africa, birds called oxpeckers live with cows, antelope, and other large animals. The oxpeckers eat ticks that attach themselves to the large animals. The large animals get rid of ticks that might harm them. The oxpeckers have a place to get food. They also get a free ride! (*See* **symbiosis.**)

If left alone, a cleared field in a forest region gradually becomes a forest. Grasses come first, then bushes and small trees. Finally, big forest trees take over.

after 2 years

Soon after a volcano killed all life, new plants from seeds poke through the ash.

Communities Change over Time If you have a vacant lot near you, you can watch how communities change. For several years, the lot may have grasses and tiny flowering plants. Then, if the lot is not mowed, you will begin to see bushes. In a few more years, you will see young trees. As more years pass, these trees grow larger. Other young trees begin to grow in the shade of the older trees. They need just a little sunlight to get started. The grasses and tiny flowers will be gone. New shrubs will take their place. Your lot will have changed from a grassy area to a young forest.

As plants in an area change, kinds of animals change. Animals that feed on grasses will not find food in a forest. Other kinds of animals will come to live in the forest.

This process of change is called *succession.* All communities go through succession. It is a slow process that takes many years.

Succession happens in lakes, too. Young lakes are very deep. Streams flowing into a lake bring soil with them. Rain running off the land around a lake also carries soil. This soil falls to the bottom of the lake. After many years, the soil fills the lake. Dry land replaces the lake, and plants begin to grow.

after 20 years

after 10 years

Many grazing animals do not eat the yellow star thistle because of its prickly spines.

Living Things Protect Themselves
Ecology is also about how living things protect themselves. You probably know how bees protect themselves. Many insects have stingers. Jellyfish, too, have stingers. Bobcats and tigers protect themselves with their teeth and claws. Skunks protect themselves with their scent. Some snakes have poison in their bites. Porcupines have sharp spines, and elk have sharp hooves and antlers.

Some animals are protected by their color or shape. A flounder is a fish that is very flat. It is also speckled. When it lies on the ocean floor, it looks like the sand and rocks. Anything chasing the flounder has trouble seeing it. The praying mantis is an insect that lives on plants. Birds like to eat it. But its thin, green body looks like the stems of the plants it rests on. It is hard for birds to see it. (*See* **camouflage.**)

Plants have ways to protect themselves, too. Rosebushes and raspberry bushes have thorns. Poison ivy leaves contain an oil that gives you an itchy rash. The roots of some other plants put poisons into the soil. These poisons kill plants that grow nearby. Some plants have poisons in their seeds. Animals learn not to eat these seeds.

Things That Are Not Alive Where certain things will live depends not only on other living things but also on several things that are not alive. One of these nonliving things is soil. Some soils are rich and deep. Many plants, such as grasses and hardwood

trees, grow well in this kind of soil. Other soils are thin and not very rich. Pine trees and their relatives can grow in these soils.

The amount of water in a place affects what lives there. Places with lots of water have many different kinds of plants and animals. Hardwood forests have lots of water. Marshes also have lots of water. Some places have very little water. The plants and animals that live in these places do not need much water. Cacti, rattlesnakes, and kangaroo rats live where there is little water. Where there is no water at all, living things cannot survive.

Temperature is another thing that affects where living things are found. Palm trees, lizards, and most monkeys live where it is warm. Polar bears, reindeer, and lemmings live where it is cold. Many birds spend summer in one place and winter in another place. This keeps them in warm areas all year.

Cycles in Nature Earth is like a spaceship. In space, there is no place to get supplies. The crew on a spaceship takes everything they need when they leave Earth. Everything that living things on Earth need must also come from the earth.

Living things use carbon, hydrogen, oxygen, and nitrogen to build their bodies. There are limited amounts of these elements on Earth. Why don't we run out of them? Think about cans. You can recycle them so they can be used again. The elements that living things need are also recycled.

Bacteria and fungi are sometimes called "nature's garbage collectors." They break down the bodies of living things that have died. When they do this important job, they also recycle elements. Bacteria and fungi release the elements in dead things. The elements return to the air and the soil. Plants use these elements to make food and grow. When animals eat the plants, they get the elements from the plants. When animals eat other animals, they, too, get the elements they need. When any of these living things die, the bacteria and fungi repeat the cycle.

Water is always evaporating from oceans and lakes. Water vapor is condensing into clouds and falling as rain or snow. This is one of many cycles in nature.

The ecology of earth is fascinating. It is a study of all the different ways living things get along together. It explains how communities change over time. It describes the cycles that give living things the materials they need to live and grow. And it helps us see how special each kind of living thing is.

See also **animal; biome;** and **environment.**

economics

Economics is the study of buying and selling, of earning money, and of paying for the things we buy. The word *economics* comes from an ancient Greek word meaning "housekeeping."

Every family knows something about economics. Money comes in, and it must be spent to pay for things the family needs. Some pays for housing and food. Some pays for clothing. Some pays for transportation. The family may have some money left over. They can save it, or spend it on a fun thing, such as a vacation.

In every household, someone must keep track of the money that comes in and goes out. Sometimes, a family has to pay out more money than it brings in. When that happens it must use money from savings, or it must borrow money.

Business Economics Businesses, too, need to use economics. For example, a company that makes and sells cars sells thousands of cars each day. It must get enough money from the cars it sells to pay for many things. It must pay for the steel and other materials that went into the cars. It must pay all the workers who helped put the cars together. It must also pay to keep its offices and factories warm and comfortable.

Planning how to spend an allowance is a first lesson in economics.

Governments get money for projects from taxes (top). Small businesses get money from selling things or services (bottom).

After it pays all its expenses, a company wants to have some money left over. This money is called its *profit*. The company may use some of its profits to make the business grow. For example, it may buy new factory machines. The rest of the profits go to the owners of the company.

Government Economics Governments *tax* people and business—collect sums of money from them based on how much money they make or how much they spend to buy things. Governments then use the money to provide services. For example, a town government runs schools, has a fire department and a police department, and keeps roads repaired. If people want more

services from the government, then they have to pay more taxes.

Economic Systems In some countries, each business decides what things to sell and how much to charge for them. This is called a *free-market system* or *capitalist system*. In other countries, the government owns all the businesses. It decides what things to make and how much to charge. This is called a *controlled-market system* or *socialist system*.

The United States practices a capitalist economic system, but the government regulates—controls—some businesses. Most governments today use a combination of the capitalist and socialist systems.

Ecuador, *see* South America

Edison, Thomas Alva

In 1847, when Thomas Edison was born, there were no record players, no movies, not even light bulbs. These were just a few of the things Edison invented that changed the way we all live.

Tom went to school for only three months, but he loved reading—especially about science and electricity. By the time he was nine, he had decided to be an inventor.

He needed money for books and equipment, so he went to work on the railroad when he was 12. He sold newspapers and snacks on the train. To make more money, he started his own newspaper, the *Weekly Herald.* He spent so much time working that he was too tired to experiment in his laboratory when he got home at night. He solved this problem by moving his laboratory into one of the train's baggage cars. He could experiment when he was not busy selling.

When Tom was 15, he rescued a small boy on the train tracks. The boy's father rewarded Tom by teaching him to operate a telegraph machine. Railroads used these machines to send messages from station to station. Tom soon became one of the best and fastest telegraph operators in the United States.

Edison moved to New York City in 1868. There, he earned a good living by repairing electric machinery. Within a few months, he was making even more money, from his first successful invention. This was a machine for reporting prices from the stock market. He quit his job and concentrated on inventing. His inventions ranged from waxed paper to a copying machine. By 1876, Edison had enough money to buy Menlo Park, a piece of land in New Jersey. On it, he built a big wooden building that he called his "Invention Factory." He hired helpers, but he still worked hard—20 hours each day.

In 1877, Edison invented the phonograph. People began calling him the "Wizard of Menlo Park." A year later, he began work on the electric light bulb. His first bulbs burned out quickly, but he kept trying. In 1879, he made a light bulb that glowed for more than 40 hours. He had succeeded at last.

After the light bulb, Edison worked on many other inventions. His most special one was "The Secret of Room 5." It was the first movie.

During his life, Edison got patents for over 1,000 inventions, but he is probably best known for the light bulb. He died in 1931, at the age of 84.

Thomas Edison developed hundreds of electrical devices. He is best known for inventing a practical light bulb so people could light their homes electrically.

movie projector

phonograph

light bulb

stock ticker

eel

Eels are fish with long, snakelike bodies. Most kinds grow to be about a meter (3 feet) long. Eels can breathe through their gills, but usually they breathe through their skin. Their skin is thick and slimy. Most kinds of eels do not have scales.

Many kinds of eels live their entire lives in the sea. Other kinds, called *freshwater eels,* spend most of their adult lives in freshwater rivers or lakes. There are freshwater eels in both North America and Europe.

When it is time to lay their eggs, freshwater eels stop eating and begin to swim toward the sea. They may travel thousands of miles before they reach their breeding grounds far out in the ocean. After they lay their eggs, they die.

A female eel may lay millions of eggs at one time. The eggs are so tiny that they can be seen only through a microscope. The baby eels—*larvae*—that hatch from the eggs do not look like adult eels. They look like thin ribbons that light can shine right through.

Gradually, the larvae grow and begin to look like adult eels. The freshwater eels soon begin their long swim to rivers and lakes. Ocean currents may carry them to the mouth of a river in North America or Europe. But then they must begin a long, uphill swim to their freshwater home.

Freshwater eels are very good climbers. Some can even climb out of the water and travel over land to find a new pond or stream. They may also climb some dams! They wriggle and jump until they reach the top of the dam. If they slip down, they try again and again until they succeed.

Adult eels usually spend the day in rock crevices or under rocks in water. Sometimes, they will take a swim or even crawl out of the water to lie in the sunshine. Eels are most active at night, when they come out to eat. They eat fish, insects, and other animals.

In Europe, eels are an important food. The meat has a strong, fishy taste. Eels are less popular as food in North America.

Some eels can be dangerous. Moray eels grow to be more than 4 meters (13 feet) long. They live in the Mediterranean Sea and in oceans near the equator. Morays have powerful jaws and very sharp teeth. They will attack and bite anything that disturbs them. People who swim and dive in places where morays live have to be careful not to disturb these creatures. The meat of the moray eel is poisonous.

See also **fish** and **electric fish.**

Large moray eels are sometimes thought of as sea monsters. They live in warm seas.

The blue ribbon eel has such a flat, long body that it scarcely looks alive.

Salmon eggs are partly clear. Inside, you can see the tiny fish growing.

egg

An egg is a special cell that forms inside a female animal. A baby animal develops from the egg. Many animals—such as amphibians, birds, and insects—lay eggs that develop outside the mother's body. Many others—such as dogs, horses, and people—develop their eggs inside their bodies. (*See* **birth** and **reproduction**.)

Before a baby animal can develop, a male sperm cell must join the female egg cell. This is called *fertilization*. Many kinds of animals *mate*—the male deposits sperm inside the female's body. Other animals, such as most fish, do not mate. Instead, the male fertilizes the eggs after the female lays them.

Most fish produce thousands of tiny eggs at once, but very few survive. Most are eaten by other fish or other animals. The same thing happens to most of the eggs of frogs and toads. A few fish, such as guppies, give birth to live young.

Turtles, alligators, crocodiles, and most snakes lay eggs. Their shells are often leathery, not hard. The mother does not keep them warm. Instead, the sun often keeps them at the right temperature.

The eggs of most mammals develop inside the mother's body. The two exceptions are the duckbill platypus and the spiny anteater. These two unusual Australian mammals lay eggs with leathery shells.

All birds lay eggs. A bird's egg has a hard shell that helps protect the egg before it hatches. Inside, the yellow yolk provides food for the developing bird. Birds' eggs have to be kept warm. Usually, the mother or father bird sits on them. But modern chicken farms keep the eggs warm in electric warmers called *incubators*. The hens go back to the job of laying more eggs.

Birds' eggs come in many colors. Most are oval in shape. Usually, the bigger the bird, the bigger the egg, but this is not always true. For example, the kiwi—a bird found in New Zealand—has a very big egg for its size.

When we think of eggs, we usually think of chicken eggs. They are a popular food sold in almost every grocery store. We scramble, fry, boil, or bake them, and we eat them at breakfast, lunch, or dinner. We use them to make omelets, sandwiches, cakes, custards, sauces, and even some drinks, such as eggnog. For Easter, we color them.

People also eat duck eggs. Tiny quail eggs are a Chinese specialty. In Africa, people eat the largest egg of all, the egg of the ostrich. Fish eggs, called *roe*, are processed to make caviar—one of the world's most expensive foods.

A hummingbird egg is a little larger than a pea. An ostrich egg may weigh 3 pounds.

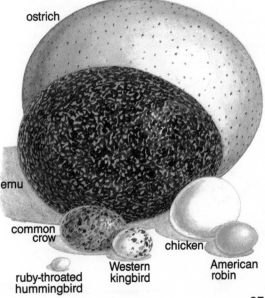

ostrich
emu
common crow
chicken
Western kingbird
American robin
ruby-throated hummingbird

Egypt

Capital: Cairo
Area: 386,660 square miles (1,001,449 square kilometers)
Population (1985): about 49,133,500
Official language: Arabic

Egypt is a large, ancient country in the northeast corner of Africa. The Sinai Peninsula, in southwestern Asia, is part of Egypt, too. Nearly the entire country is desert. The Nile River, the longest river in the world, flows north through Egypt to the Mediterranean Sea. Most Egyptians live in the Nile valley or on its delta. A few live in *oases*—small fertile areas around a source of water. Oases are scattered over the desert.

Most Egyptians are farmers. They grow rice, fruits, vegetables, and wheat. Cotton is an important export crop. The soil along the Nile is very fertile. But farming methods have not changed for thousands of years.

Egypt gets very little rain. It depends on the Nile River and on the reservoir behind the Aswan High Dam for its water. The Aswan High Dam also provides electric power for homes and factories.

More of Egypt's people are moving to the cities. Cairo, Egypt's capital and the largest

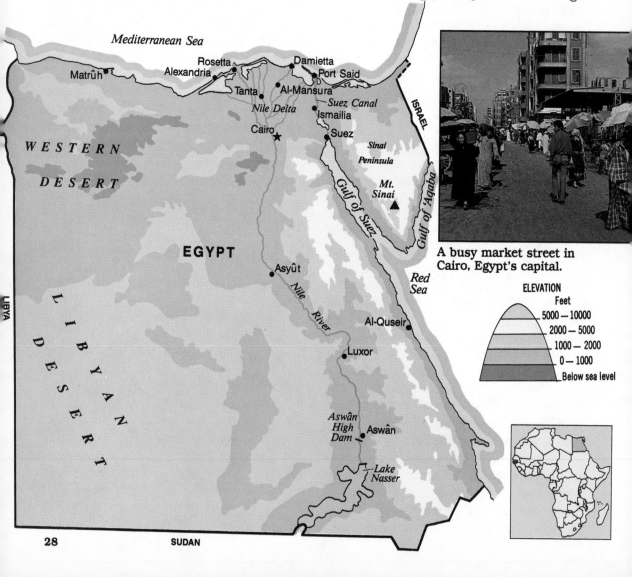

A busy market street in Cairo, Egypt's capital.

ELEVATION
Feet
5000 — 10000
2000 — 5000
1000 — 2000
0 — 1000
Below sea level

city in Africa, is on the Nile, in northern Egypt. The many factories in or near Cairo produce textiles, glass, iron and steel products, and refrigerators. Alexandria, Egypt's second-largest city, is a Mediterranean port. (*See* **Alexandria.**)

The Suez Canal separates the main part of Egypt from the Sinai Peninsula. The canal links the Mediterranean with the Red Sea and the Indian Ocean. It is an important shipping route.

The ancient Egyptians had one of the world's first great civilizations. It lasted almost 3,000 years. Today, people still visit Egypt to see the Great Sphinx, the pyramids, and other monuments from Egypt's magnificent past. (*See* **Egypt, ancient.**)

For centuries afterward, Egypt was ruled by foreign powers. It became part of the Roman Empire in 30 B.C. Then, in the 600s, the Arabs conquered Egypt and introduced the Islamic religion. The Turks ruled Egypt from the 1500s to the 1800s. By the 1880s, it was controlled by Great Britain. Egypt became an independent country again in 1922. Its official name is now the Arab Republic of Egypt.

In 1947, the state of Israel was created. It bordered Egypt in the Sinai Peninsula. Egypt and other Arab nations were against the founding of Israel. Egypt has been at war with Israel four times, most recently in 1973. In 1978, U.S. president Jimmy Carter brought Egyptian president Anwar el-Sadat together with Israeli leaders to discuss their problems. As a result, Egypt and Israel signed a peace treaty in 1979.

See also **Middle East.**

Egypt, ancient

Almost 5,000 years before the founding of the United States, the people of Egypt built a powerful civilization. The Egyptians were the first people in the world to have a national government. They built cities, temples, and pyramids that are wonders of engineering. They also invented a method of

The sphinx and pyramids (background) were built at Giza almost 4,500 years ago.

writing, and made important discoveries in mathematics and medicine.

An Unusual Land Geography played an important part in Egypt's development. Ancient Egypt covered a large area west of the Red Sea. Almost all of this land was part of the Sahara Desert, which stretches across northern Africa. Life would have been almost impossible if not for the Nile River. The Nile is the world's longest river. It rises in the mountains to the south of Egypt and winds its way north through the country, emptying into the Mediterranean Sea.

Every summer, the Nile overflowed its banks and left behind rich, black soil on the land. This made the land so fertile that Egyptian farmers could grow enough grain, vegetables, and fruit to feed all the people. Almost everyone in Egypt lived along the Nile. Cliffs and desert bordered the farmland of the Nile River Valley and provided protection against invaders. This allowed the country to develop in peace.

Rulers and Religion At first, the Egyptians lived in separate communities along the Nile. Then, around 3100 B.C., a ruler named Menes united the country and built a capital city named Memphis. Menes was the first Egyptian *pharaoh*—king.

The pharaoh owned most of the land in Egypt. Government officials and priests carried out his orders. Taxes were collected to support the government and set up an army. The Egyptians felt that the pharaoh was a god who had the power to keep their country strong.

A pyramid was a tomb for a king (above).
Inside the pyramid was a burial room (right).

The Egyptians believed in many gods and goddesses. One of the most important of their gods was Re, god of the sun. Another important god was Osiris, god of the dead. The Egyptians believed in a life after death. They believed that when they died, they would go to a pleasant place that they called the *underworld.*

In order to enjoy life after death, however, people would need their physical bodies. For this reason, the Egyptians developed the science of *embalming*—preserving the body with chemicals and other substances. The embalmed body, wrapped in layers of cloth, was called a *mummy.* (*See* **mummy.**)

Egyptian tombs contained not only mummies but also weapons, food, dishes, jewelry, cosmetics, and other things the dead might want to use in the underworld. The tombs of the pharaohs were filled with gold and precious jewels. The most famous of these tombs are the pyramids built near Memphis. Another well-known burial place of the pharaohs is the Valley of the Kings, near the city of Thebes. Over the years, robbers have broken into the tombs and stolen many objects, including mummies. In the 1920s, scientists found the first royal tomb that had never been broken into. It belonged to a pharaoh named Tutankhamen. (*See* **Tutankhamen** and **pyramid.**)

People Egyptian society had four different classes. The royal family and the nobles were the highest class. Next were the traders, artists, and craftsmen. The third class was made up of workers, such as farmers. The slaves belonged to the lowest class.

Family life was very important in ancient Egypt. Children were loved and enjoyed by their parents. At first, men ruled the family. Later, women gained equality. Both sons and daughters could inherit property from their parents. Women of the royal family sometimes had great influence in the government of Egypt. The most famous of the Egyptian queens was Cleopatra, who became queen in 51 B.C. and ruled together with her brother, Ptolemy. (*See* **Cleopatra.**)

Most Egyptians were farmers, but each community had its craftsmen. They wove cloth or made jewelry and pottery in their shops. Many communities also had shipyards. Egyptian traders sailed to places in Asia, Africa, and Europe. The traders did not use money to buy products from other peoples. Instead, they swapped their own goods for the goods of others. This way of trading was called *bartering.*

Ancient Egyptians made pictures to record their history. These pictures from a tomb in Luxor show Egyptians at work growing and transporting their crops.

Art and Learning   About 4,500 years ago, the Egyptians developed a form of picture writing called *hieroglyphics*. Hieroglyphics were painted on the walls of temples and carved in stone. These writings were preserved by the dry climate. We have learned a great deal about ancient Egypt from reading them. (*See* **hieroglyphics**.)

The Egyptians also created a kind of paper from the papyrus plant. The English word *paper* comes from the word *papyrus.*

One of the most important Egyptian writings was the *Book of the Dead.* It contained prayers to help the spirits of the dead travel to the underworld. The Egyptians also wrote hymns, love poems, and books teaching people the proper way to behave.

The Egyptians were excellent builders. They were probably the first people to build with stone. They built huge statues of pharaohs and temples to the gods. One such temple was built at Karnak in the 1200s B.C. to honor the sun god. It has columns 78 feet (23 meters) high—the largest columned hall ever built. Thousands of people, many of them slaves, worked all their lives to build the temples, statues, and pyramids. The Bible tells the story of how the Egyptian pharoah forced the Jews to work as slaves until Moses finally led them out of Egypt to freedom.

The Egyptians decorated their buildings with paintings and statues of the gods and the pharaohs. Many paintings also showed ordinary people. But Egyptian artists did not let the faces they painted express feelings. They felt that this gave their artwork a look of power and dignity.

The scientific discoveries of the Egyptians included a system of measuring land. This skill, called *surveying,* was used each year to set up the boundaries of farms after the Nile River flooded and washed them away. The Egyptians also used fractions, and worked out some of the basic rules of algebra and geometry. This helped them cut stone blocks of exactly the right size for their temples and pyramids. The ancient Egyptians understood the heart's role in the human body.

The Fall of Egypt   The civilization of ancient Egypt lasted about 2,500 years. During this time, Egypt's borders changed as different lands came under its control. Egypt began to lose power between 1500 and 1000 B.C., when other peoples started using iron. Egypt had no natural supply of iron, and lost battles against armies that had iron weapons. The hot, dry air and sands of Egypt, however, preserved the art, writings, and tombs of this ancient people, so that their story is known today.

See also **Egypt**.

Einstein, Albert

Many people consider Albert Einstein the most important scientist of the 1900s. His ideas about light, space, time, matter, energy, and gravity changed the science of physics.

Born in Ulm, Germany, in 1879, young Albert did not seem very much like a genius. He did not do very well in school, and later could not find a job teaching in a college. He went to work at the Swiss Patent Office, but his real work was developing his ideas.

In 1905, Einstein sent several remarkable papers to a physics journal. In one, he showed that light was both a particle and a wave. This idea helped people understand atoms, and Einstein was given the Nobel Prize for Physics in 1921. In two other papers, he was the first to show that atoms really existed. He made it possible to calculate the size of individual atoms. (*See* **atom**.)

Two more papers presented the beginning of Einstein's famous *theory of relativity.* The *special theory* of relativity says that motion, matter, and time are related to each other. The famous formula $E = mc^2$ is one of the results of the special theory. E stands for energy, m stands for mass, and c stands for the speed of light. Since the speed of light is very great, the formula means that even a small mass can be turned into a lot of energy. Einstein, a kind and peaceful man, hoped atomic energy would help people. He was not happy that his idea led to the atomic bomb.

The theory of relativity has another part, which Einstein presented in 1915, ten years after his papers about the special theory. The *general theory* explains gravity. One reason Einstein became so famous is that his theory of gravity improved upon Sir Isaac Newton's theory of gravity. (*See* **Newton, Sir Isaac.**)

In 1905, Einstein became a doctor of philosophy. Soon, many universities wanted him. In 1919, his prediction that light rays could be bent by gravity was proved. He became the most famous scientist in the world.

In 1933, Einstein came to live in the United States. He worked at the Institute for Advanced Studies in Princeton, New Jersey. There he continued searching for new and creative answers about gravity, matter, and energy until his death in 1955. In his last years, he struggled with problems that almost no one else even tried to solve. Scientists now see that these problems are very important, and many physicists are trying to solve them.

Einstein (left) explained that what direction an object is moving and how fast it is going may depend on where it is measured from (right).

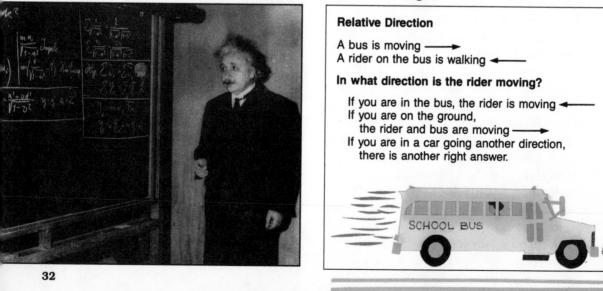

Relative Direction

A bus is moving ⟶
A rider on the bus is walking ⟵

In what direction is the rider moving?

If you are in the bus, the rider is moving ⟵
If you are on the ground,
the rider and bus are moving ⟶
If you are in a car going another direction,
there is another right answer.

SCHOOL BUS

Dwight Eisenhower, known as "Ike," was an army general and a popular president.

Eisenhower, Dwight D.

Dwight David Eisenhower was the 34th president of the United States, serving from 1953 to 1961. As a general during World War II, he became famous by leading the fight for victory in Europe.

Born in 1890, in Denison, Texas, young "Ike" actually grew up in Abilene, Kansas. In high school, he was a good student and a star football player. But his family could not afford to send him to college. He went instead to the U.S. Military Academy at West Point, New York, where the government would pay for his education.

His years at West Point convinced Eisenhower that he wanted to spend his life as a soldier. Soon after his graduation in 1915, the United States entered World War I. Eisenhower hoped to lead men into battle, but instead spent the war training tank battalions. In the years that followed, he served in many different posts.

In late 1941, the United States entered World War II. Eisenhower was an unknown colonel, but his abilities soon skyrocketed him to high rank and fame. He was made a general. Then he was named supreme commander of all the forces fighting against Germany and Italy in Europe.

Eisenhower had a great talent for planning attacks and for getting people to work well together. He gave people confidence in themselves. His wartime leadership won him friends all over the world. After victory in Europe in 1945, he received a hero's welcome at home.

When Eisenhower ran for president in 1952, his popularity swept him into the White House. At that time, U.S. troops were fighting in Korea. Eisenhower went to Korea and succeeded in getting a ceasefire. This eventually led to the war's end.

Eisenhower remained popular throughout two terms as president. During the "Eisenhower Years," business boomed and many jobs were created. In 1957, Eisenhower sent federal troops to Little Rock, Arkansas, to enforce laws saying that black students could go to school with white students. In 1958, the United States launched its first space satellite, *Explorer* 1. People were still shouting "I LIKE IKE!" when Eisenhower left office.

In 1961, Eisenhower retired to his farm near the Civil War battlefield of Gettysburg, Pennsylvania. He died in 1969 and is buried near his boyhood home in Abilene.

electric appliances

In the morning, are you awakened by a clock radio? Do you pop bread into the toaster? Do you brush your teeth with an electric toothbrush? Do you dry your hair with a hair dryer? After school, do you go to the refrigerator for a snack, then switch on the stereo, television, or VCR? At night, do you snuggle under an electric blanket?

Electric appliances make work easier and faster. They can also entertain us, make us more comfortable, and protect our health.

Some electric appliances, such as the VCR, are recent inventions. Color television and stereo recording are older. They were invented in the 1950s. Electric fans, vacuum

Before electric appliances, people had to carry water and wood to their house, cook on a wood stove, wash clothes by hand, and preserve their own food. Even the youngest members of a family helped with household chores.

cleaners, and radios have been around since the 1920s. But before people could use these appliances, electricity had to be available in their homes. In the United States, most homes had electricity before 1940.

At one time, many homes had servants to help with the housework. Today's "servants" are often electric appliances. It used to take an entire day to do a family's laundry. Now, whenever there are a few clothes to wash, we run them through a washer and dryer. Instead of cutting ice from a frozen pond, we get it from the freezer. Electric food processors speed up food preparation.

Kinds of Appliances Some electric appliances use electricity to power a motor. Fans, electric mixers, electric can openers, and electric razors have motors. Other electrical appliances use electricity to produce heat. These include electric blankets, toasters, and irons. Some appliances do both. An electric clothes dryer, for example, needs a motor to turn the drum and heat to dry the clothes. (*See* **electric motor**.)

Most electric appliances get their electricity from wall outlets. But in order for these appliances to work in all households, every home must have the same kind of electric current coming from the outlet. The United States set up a common current for the whole country in the 1930s. Other countries, however, use different currents. Travelers can buy *adaptors* so their appliances will work with different currents. Many travelers prefer to carry battery-operated appliances, which do not need to be plugged in.

With electric appliances, chores can be done quickly and easily. A refrigerator keeps foods fresh, and an automatic stove or microwave oven cooks quickly. Families have more leisure time to do the things they enjoy.

Many appliances, such as portable radios and tape recorders, may use either batteries or wall outlets. Some battery-operated appliances are plugged into a wall outlet when not in use. This recharges their batteries. When you use these appliances, you remove them from the outlet and carry them anywhere, even outdoors. Mixers, razors, and small vacuum cleaners can be used this way.

Appliance Safety In the United States, the Underwriter's Laboratory tests appliances for safety. Appliances with a "UL" label are safe to use.

Electric appliances use various amounts of *amperes* and *watts.* Amperes measure the rate of flow of electricity. Watts measure the amount of electricity. Most household electric appliances use either 15 or 20 amperes.

An appliance labeled "20 amperes" should not be plugged into an outlet that delivers only 15 amperes. A light bulb that requires 100 watts should not be used in a lamp designed for only 75 watts. It is safe to use a lower-watt bulb, but not a higher-watt bulb.

To avoid electric shock, you should keep electric appliances and their cords away from water. Make sure your hands are dry when you turn an appliance on or off. Inspect the cords to make sure they are not worn out. This is especially important for older appliances with old-fashioned cords. Appliances usually come from the store with instructions on how to use them. Most appliances are safe if you follow the directions and use them properly.

See also **electricity** and **electric power.**

electric fish

Some fish can produce electricity. They use the electricity to catch food, fight enemies, and find their way through the water.

The fish that produce the strongest electricity are electric eels, electric catfish, and electric rays. Some of these fish can be quite large. Electric eels, for example, may be more than 180 centimeters (6 feet) long.

The electric eel lives in rivers of South America. This fish has a long body like an eel, but is not a true eel. The electric organs are in the tail, which makes up most of the body. These organs produce two kinds of electric discharge. As the fish moves about, it gives off a weak but regular pulse. This helps the electric eel find its way. The electric eel can also give off a high-voltage discharge. It uses this to stun or kill prey—the creatures it eats—and to fight enemies. Usually, it kills frogs or other fish. But its electricity is powerful enough to knock out a horse.

Electric catfish live in rivers and lakes in tropical Africa. These fish have plump bodies and three pairs of whiskerlike feelers around the mouth. The electric organ is in muscles under the skin. Electric discharges are used to catch food and to fight enemies.

Electric rays are odd-looking fish. They have an almost circular shape, with a short, slender tail. One kind looks like a circle that has been cut in half. Electric rays live on the bottoms of all tropical and temperate seas.

They have two electric organs, one on each side of the head. They catch fish and other small animals by pouncing and wrapping their fins around the prey. Then they use the electricity to stun the prey. Electric rays also use their electricity to find their way along the ocean bottom and to locate prey.

Another interesting electric fish is the elephant-snout fish. It lives in muddy lakes and streams in Africa. Its electric organs are in the base of its tail. The fish surrounds itself with an electric field. If anything enters this field, the fish is alerted. This is very useful, because the fish has poor eyesight.

The stargazer is an electric fish found in the eastern United States. It has two eyes on top of its head, and its mouth, too, faces up. The stargazer's electric organs have developed from eye muscle and are located right behind its eyes.

electricity

What do a TV picture, lightning, and clinging clothes from a dryer have in common? All of them are caused by tiny electrically charged particles called *electrons*. The flow or movement of electrons is often called *electricity*. Electric charges cause clothes to cling. Electrical energy makes TVs work. It makes electric motors hum and electric doorbells ring. To understand how electricity works, we have to look closely at the tiny particles that make up all matter.

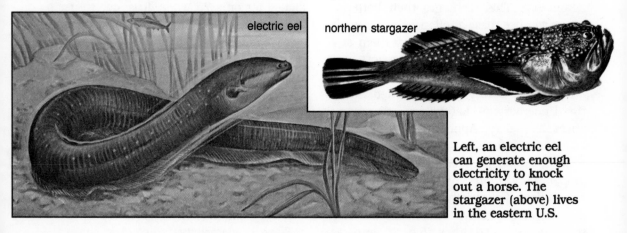

electric eel

northern stargazer

Left, an electric eel can generate enough electricity to knock out a horse. The stargazer (above) lives in the eastern U.S.

Static electricity from a Van de Graaff generator makes these girls' hair stand on end without hurting them. Lightning (above) has enough electricity to kill a person.

Static Electricity All matter is made of atoms, tiny particles held together by electric forces. Inside each atom are positively charged protons and negatively charged electrons. They are attracted to each other. But the tinier electrons can pull away from the protons and become free. Where there are many free electrons, negative charges collect. The protons they left behind form an area of positive charges. A buildup of positive or negative charges is known as *static electricity*. (*See* **atom**.)

If you brush your hair on a dry day, you may see sparks or hear a crackling sound. This happens because as you brush, many free electrons gather in your hair. Your brush does not have as many negative charges, so the charges from your hair jump to the brush.

Sometimes, there is a massive buildup of electrons in a cloud. You see lightning when the electrons are finally *discharged*—released—to the ground. (*See* **lightning.**)

In every case, objects that have many negative charges push each other away. But a positively charged object and a negatively charged object will be attracted to each other. They will cling together.

Some kinds of objects seem to attract electrons more strongly. If you walk across a wool rug and then touch a metal doorknob, you may get a shock. The electrons are so attracted to the metal that they jump from your hand to the doorknob. A metal doorknob is an example of what is called a *conductor*. It easily conducts—carries— electric charges. Most conductors have many free electrons. Objects that generally do not conduct charges are called *insulators*.

Electricity in Circuits A bolt of lighting is a dramatic show of energy. But usually this energy spreads into the ground without being put to good use. To put electrical energy to use, we must control it. This usually means channeling it into an electric circuit.

If a negatively charged region and a positively charged region are joined by a conductor, any free electrons from the negative side tend to move through the conductor. This causes a flow of electrons, called a *current*. The electrons flow in waves along a path called a *circuit*.

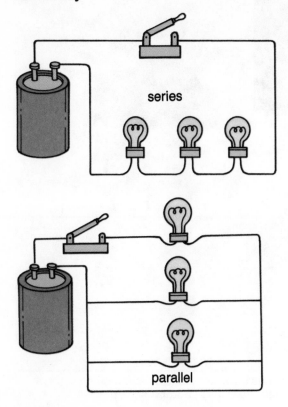

series

parallel

If a bulb in a series circuit burns out, all the bulbs go out. In a parallel circuit, the other bulbs stay lighted.

In order for a circuit to be useful, it needs several connected parts. First, there is a source of electrical charge, such as a battery. A battery converts chemical energy into electrical energy. Second, there is something in the circuit to use the electricity, such as a light or motor. Third, there is a switch to open and close the circuit. When the switch is on, the circuit is closed—it is complete. The battery begins pumping the electrons through the circuit. It is the moving electrons that can do the work. They will cause the metal inside the light to glow, or turn the shaft of an electric motor. If the switch is off, the circuit is broken. Once the circuit is broken, no charge can flow.

There are different ways of connecting circuits. In a *series circuit,* there is only one path for the electrons to take. In a *parallel circuit,* there are many wires. They provide different paths for the electrons to take. The current divides into the various paths in the circuit.

Most circuits are made from copper or aluminum wire. Copper and aluminum are especially good conductors. Today's modern electronic tools, however, do not use wires. Instead, metal paint is used to print a tiny circuit on a board. This printed circuit is much smaller than a circuit with wires.

Where Our Electrical Energy Comes From When you plug in an electric hair dryer or a VCR, you say that you are using electricity. But really you are using electric power. The source of this power is not a battery but a generator. Large generators supply huge quantities of electric power to the area where you live.

People usually say a generator "produces electricity." But what a generator really does is change some other kind of energy into electrical energy. (*See* **electric power.**)

Electrical Energy at Work in Your Home Electrical energy can be changed into other kinds of energy to make our lives easier. An electric toaster, for example, changes electrical energy into heat energy to toast bread. Many appliances have an electric motor that changes electrical energy to mechanical energy. (*See* **electric appliances.**)

A toaster turns electricity into heat, a fan turns it into motion, and a light bulb turns it into light.

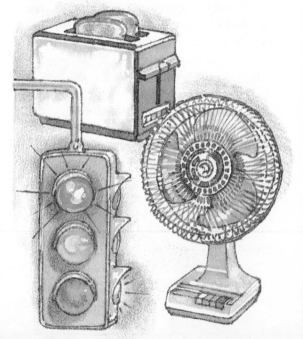

WATCH OUT FOR ELECTRICAL HAZARDS

Never plug too many appliances into one electrical socket.

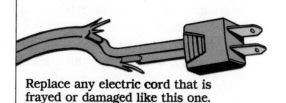

Replace any electric cord that is frayed or damaged like this one.

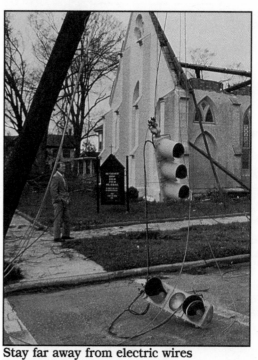

Stay far away from electric wires that have been knocked down.

A television set uses electrons to produce the picture we see. A television, as well as a computer screen, contains a very important electronic device. This device is known as a CRT—cathode-ray tube. This is a glass tube in which electrons are given off in a steady stream. The stream of electrons changes as it receives electronic signals like those broadcast over the air. When the electrons hit the screen, they glow, producing the pattern we see as a picture. (*See* **television** and **electronics.**)

When using any appliance or electronic device, it is important to think of safety. Wiring should be in good condition, not frayed or damaged. Take care not to plug too many appliances into one circuit. Every home has fuses or circuit breakers to prevent circuits from overloading. If they are overloaded, the power will turn off. Never use appliances near water or with wet hands. When you are finished using an electrical appliance turn it off. Be a responsible energy user.

electric motor

Try to imagine life without electric motors. You would hear less music, because electric motors keep turntables turning. Summertime would feel much hotter, because air conditioners are run by electric motors. Clothes would be harder to clean, because electric motors run washing machines and dryers. (*See* **electric appliances.**)

Electric motors turn electrical energy into mechanical energy. The electrical energy may come from a wall socket in your home, or from a battery. Electricity provides the energy in electric motors, just as gasoline provides energy in most car motors.

There are millions of electric motors in the world. Small electric motors run many appliances. Large electric motors power trains and factory machinery. All electric motors work on the same principle. Electricity provides energy for magnets in the motor. Then, magnetic forces create motion.

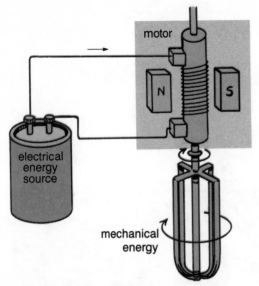

An electric motor turns electricity into mechanical power. Here the power turns an electric mixer.

To understand how an electric motor works, think of a turntable. When you turn on the turntable, electric current goes to the motor. The current causes iron bars in the motor to become magnets. Strong magnetic forces turn a rod called the *drive shaft* in the middle of the motor. The drive shaft is connected to the turntable. When the drive shaft turns, the turntable turns—and you can play a record. (*See* **magnetism**.)

A small electric motor in a phonograph provides the power to turn the turntable.

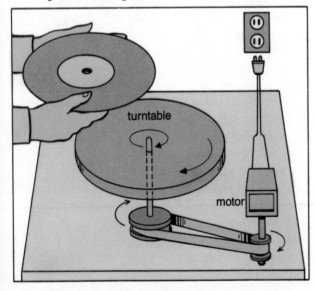

The big advantage of electric motors is that they do not create exhaust fumes like gasoline engines do. Their big disadvantage is that electric motors need a constant source of electricity. Electric cars would be an improvement over gasoline-powered cars except for this disadvantage. You would not be able to drive very far in a car that always had to be plugged into a wall socket! So electric cars must run on batteries. With today's batteries, electric automobiles can travel only about 100 miles before their batteries have to be recharged.

Train engines get their electricity directly from electric power plants. Engines on diesel trains run generators that make electricity. The electricity then powers the motors that run the train. Subways and other trains use a different system. They get electricity from overhead wires or a "third rail" that lies beside the tracks. These electric train engines are always "plugged in." (*See* **generator**.)

See also **electricity** and **electric power**.

electric power

In 1879, Thomas Edison found a practical way to produce bright light from electricity. His invention of the light bulb may not seem all that special today. After all, you are used to seeing light bulbs around your home. Yet Edison's light bulb opened the present era of electric power. (*See* **Edison, Thomas Alva**.)

Electric motors and other devices that use electricity were around before the light bulb. But these had not brought electric power into people's homes. Electric lighting was a great improvement over candles and gas or oil lamps. People quickly formed companies to provide homes with electricity. When most homes had electricity, it could be used for many other things besides lighting. Anything you plug into a wall socket—a television, a computer, a refrigerator—runs on electric power. (*See* **electric motor** and **electric appliances**.)

Not all the uses of electricity are in the home, however. Giant magnets, elevators, trains, and many other kinds of machinery use electric power. Also, many important substances, such as aluminum, could not be made cheaply without electric power.

History of Electric Power Electricity was known to the ancient Greeks. They knew that if you rubbed a hard material called *amber—elektron* in Greek—it would develop a mysterious power. The rubbed amber could pick up small bits of feather or straw. But that is all they knew about electricity, and it had no practical use.

In the 1700s, scientists became interested in electricity, but they did not have a steady source of power. They could produce electric sparks, but not a steady current. In 1800, an Italian scientist named Alessandro Volta invented the first electric cell. An electric cell changes chemical energy into electricity. A battery is made of two or more cells connected together. A battery can produce an electric current for many hours at a time. (*See* **battery**.)

With this steady source of power, scientists could finally put electricity to work. Using current from the battery, for example, they discovered an even better source of

power, the electric generator. By 1858, electric power was being used to light lamps in lighthouses as a guide for ships at sea. The same year the light bulb was invented—1879—the first electric power company began operating in California. By 1900, there were more than 3,000 electric power companies in the United States.

Electric Power Plants Most of the world's electric power comes from electric power plants. These are large "factories" that make electricity. They send electric power to homes, offices, and factories through overhead wires and underground cables.

Electric power is measured in *watts*. Most light bulbs in your home, for example, need between 25 and 150 watts of electric power to produce light. The world's electric power plants can produce more than 2 trillion watts of electric power at any one time. That is enough electricity to light up 20 billion 100-watt light bulbs!

How do electric power plants produce electric power? After the battery was invented, scientists discovered that moving wires through the space around magnets produces

The cars on this commuter train receive electric power from a third rail just to the left of the main rails. Electric motors use the electricity to move the train.

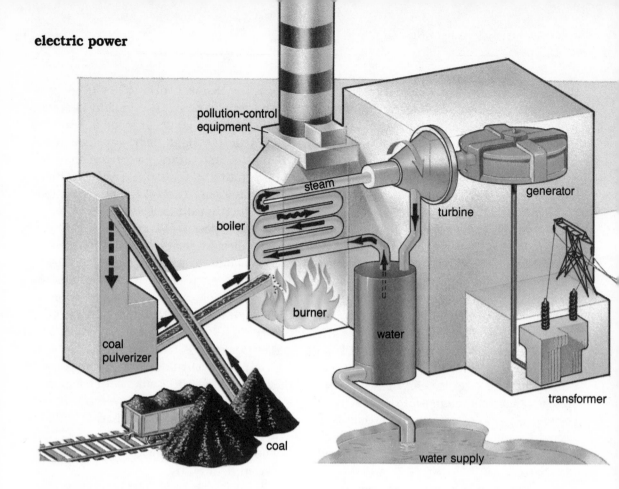

pollution-control equipment

steam

boiler

generator

turbine

coal pulverizer

burner

water

transformer

coal

water supply

electric current in the wires. An electric generator is a machine that moves magnets past coils of copper wire. The motion produces a current in the wire. The current can then be sent out through other wires to homes and businesses. (*See* **magnetism.**)

The most common kind of electric power plants burn *fossil fuels*—oil, coal, or natural gas. Power plants that burn fossil fuels produce about two-thirds of all electric power.

Burning the fuel heats a large store of water. When the water gets very hot, it turns to steam. Steam takes much more space than water does, so pressure builds up. To get an idea of steam pressure, think of heating water in a "whistling" teapot. When the water boils, the teapot whistles. That is because steam under pressure is rushing through a small hole in the spout.

In an electric power plant, the steam is used to turn a kind of fan called a *turbine.* The turbine is connected to the electric generator. The movement of magnets inside the generator causes an electric current.

The second most common kind of electric power plant is a *nuclear* plant. Nuclear plants work much like plants that burn fossil fuels. But the fuel is not burned to produce heat. Instead, a controlled nuclear reaction generates heat. (*See* **nuclear power.**)

The third most common kind of electric power plant is a *hydroelectric* plant. *Hydro* means "water," and hydroelectric power plants get their power from moving water. About one of every ten electric power plants is a hydroelectric plant.

Hydroelectric plants are built near rivers, streams, or waterfalls. If there is no natural waterfall, a dam produces an artificial one. As water falls from one level to another, it turns a turbine. The turbine then turns an electric generator.

In windy places, giant windmills can produce enough energy to generate electricity. Solar energy—energy from the sun—can also generate electricity. Batteries use chemicals to produce electricity. (*See* **battery.**)

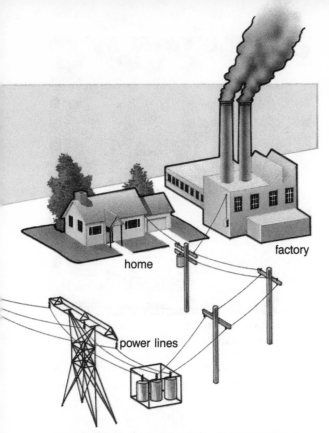

In a coal-burning power plant, steam turns a turbine, and a generator makes mechanical energy into electricity. The power is sent through lines to homes and factories.

Another device that changes chemical energy to electrical energy is the *fuel cell.* They have been used in spacecraft, but fuel cells large enough to provide electric power for a whole city are still experimental.

Transmitting Electric Power The electric current produced in a plant's generator is sent out through overhead wires or underground cables to smaller power stations. Other wires and cables carry it to homes, factories, and other places that need electricity.

When the electricity first leaves the plant, its *voltage*—electrical force—is too powerful for your home. The strength of an electric current is measured in *volts*. The number of volts in the power plant's electric current is several hundred times the voltage that comes from a wall socket in your home. When it reaches the smaller power stations, the voltage is changed by devices called *transformers*. Different electric voltages are used for different purposes. Electric trains, for example, use much higher voltage than the lights and appliances in your home.

Concerns About Electric Power One of the greatest concerns about electric power is the use of nuclear power plants. Many people worry about accidents at these plants. In an accident, dangerous radioactive substances can escape into the environment.

At one time, scientists believed that nuclear plants would supply more than half of the world's electricity. Today, however, less than one-quarter of all electric power comes from nuclear plants. Because of concerns about safety, few new nuclear plants are being built.

Many people also worry about air pollution from fuel-burning plants. But despite these concerns, almost no one is saying we should do away with electric power. Most of us would find it very hard to live in a world without electric power, the way people lived more than 100 years ago.

See also electricity.

---

electron, *see* atom

In a hydroelectric plant, falling water turns turbines to generate electricity.

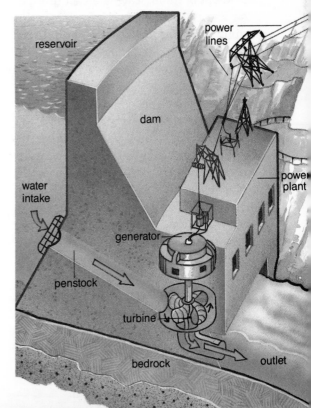

electronics

The picture on your television screen, the voice you hear on the telephone, the program you use to work at a computer—electronics makes all these possible.

Electronics is the use of electrons to carry information. This is not the same as using electricity for power, light, or heat. In those cases, the amount of electricity or its kind is important. Electronics deals with controlling the movement of electrons. In fact, the word *electronics* comes from the word *electron.*

Electrons are small parts of atoms. They are tiny electric particles. Electrons that become separated from their atoms are called *free electrons.* When they move in a stream, they can produce an electric current. Such currents provide power. (*See* **electricity.**)

Electronic appliances use electricity to receive, process, or send information. Often, they translate information into a different form. For example, television translates radio waves into a picture on a screen.

Electronic Devices The oldest electronic devices are *vacuum tubes.* The air has been pumped out of them, leaving a vacuum. The air is removed so that the electrons carrying information through the tube will not bump into air molecules. (*See* **molecule.**)

In modern electronic devices, electrons do not move through a vacuum. Instead, they move through a solid material that conducts—carries—the current. We call these devices *solid-state.* Solid-state electronic devices are smaller and lighter than vacuum tubes. They make it possible to have pocket radios, small computers, and even miniature television sets that work electronically.

The first solid-state electronic devices were *transistors.* Transistors are much smaller and lighter than vacuum tubes. Some are tinier than a dime. A transistor is made from crystals of a metal called *germanium.* Transistors are a big improvement over vacuum tubes. They need less current, they last much longer, and they are less breakable than vacuum tubes.

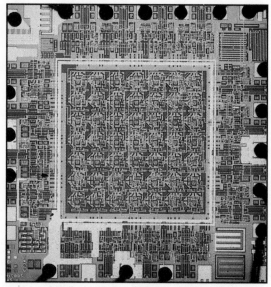

A magnified view of an integrated circuit shows pathways for electric current.

Today, we use electronic devices that are even smaller and lighter than transistors. They are called *integrated circuits,* or *chips.* A chip is made from silicon, a crystal material that is found in beach sand. The electric current travels along small pathways that are carefully etched into the silicon. Chips are used in computers and in hearing aids. They are even used in microwave ovens. (*See* **chip, computer.**)

Sending the Message In order to send information by electronics, the movement of electrons—the current—must be changed in a special way.

There are two ways to change an electric current so it can carry information. One is called the *analog* method. A good example of analog electronics is the radio. In radio broadcasting, different levels of loudness or pitch are directly changed by variations in the electric current. To understand the analog method, think about a wave of water. Each wave of water has a certain height and is a certain distance away from the next wave.

Electric current moves in waves, too. But small changes in the height and distance of the waves of electric current can have meaning. These changes carry a message. When the message reaches your radio, equipment inside it changes the current back to voices or music.

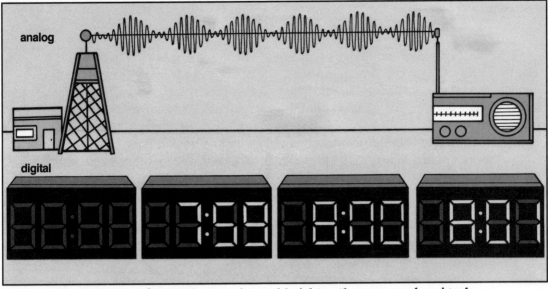

Radio waves (top) have different frequencies and heights—they are *analog* signals. The clock's lights show [digital] signals.

The other way to change an electric current is the *digital* method. Information is changed to pulses of electricity. Think of the way you might use a flashlight to send a message to a friend. Turning the light on or off would have a meaning. So would the number of flashes. You would send your message using a pattern or code of light flashes. In the same way, turning an electric current on and off in short bursts can send information, such as a telephone message. At the other end, the short bursts are changed back to voice form.

How Electronic Information Travels Telephone systems and wires, including underground and undersea cables, carry electronic information all over the world. The messages are sent digitally, so thousands of separate conversations can be sent at the same time through the same cable.

Microwave communication is another way of sending electronic information. The microwave system uses towers about 30 miles apart. Radio waves called *microwaves* are sent through the air from tower to tower. (*See* **microwave communications.**)

Fiber optics is a way of sending electronic information by using light. Pulses of light are sent through pure glass fibers much thinner than a drinking straw. These fibers are called *light guides.* The light waves stay inside the light guides because each time they strike the edge of the glass, they are reflected back into the center. The light pulses carry digital information. Fiber optics is not really part of electronics. This is because light is used to send messages instead of electrons being used. But electronic devices are used at each end to code or decode the message.

In an optic fiber, messages are pulses of light of different frequencies. A single fiber can carry many messages at once.

A great deal of electronic information is sent by satellites. Special communications satellites can receive and transmit information anywhere in the world. (*See* **communications satellite.**)

Electronics Today One of the most familiar tools for sharing and storing information today is the computer. Computers have made a big difference in all our lives. Governments, banks, schools, libraries, and even families rely on computers to store, sort, and handle many kinds of information.

Devices called *modems* link computers together by telephone, so that electronic information can be shared. Using modems, computer users can reach large "banks" of information on specific subjects. They can send messages to one another, or even play chess or other games! Businesses use modems, too. They can send charts, graphs, reports, or other important information anywhere in the world. Publishers send entire newspapers, magazines, or even books by computer to other locations to be set in type. (*See* **computer.**)

Health and medicine have also been influenced by electronics. Special electronic microscopes allow doctors to see things they could not see before. An "electronic eye," based on fiber optics, helps doctors see areas inside the human body.

Space exploration has been aided by electronics. On space shuttles, electronic equipment records and sends information and pictures to receiving stations back on earth. Modern electronic telescopes help scientists explore space from observatories here on Earth.

Some people think that one day in the future, electronics may even take the place of schools and libraries. They believe that some day everyone will be able to learn and find any information they need by using machines like computers, at home. Whether or not this really happens, electronics will continue to change the way people find and use information. Modern electronics makes more knowledge available to more people—easily and quickly.

See also **radio; television;** and **laser.**

Electronics makes it possible for two people many miles apart to play a computer game together, and for satellites to send us photos of a planet from outer space.

The shiny yellow patches in this rock are made of copper.

element

The ancient Greeks thought that everything was made from combinations of just a few simple things—elements. Different Greek thinkers had different lists of elements. But most of them listed just four—earth, air, fire, and water.

When people began to experiment with chemicals, it became clear that there were more than four elements. In 1661, an Englishman, Robert Boyle, thought over the problem. He knew that some chemicals were made from a combination of chemicals. He decided that all chemicals must be made from a few basic chemicals. He called these basic chemicals by the old Greek name—elements.

At first, it was not clear which simple chemicals were elements. It was easy to see that some metals—such as gold, iron, and mercury—were elements. But in the beginning, scientists thought air, water, and salt were also elements. Today, we know that air is not an element. It is a mixture of elements—mostly nitrogen and oxygen. We also know that water and salt are *compounds,* chemical combinations of elements. Salt, for example, is a compound of the elements sodium and chlorine. (*See* **compound.**)

We now know that 89 elements exist in nature. People have made another 20 that do not exist naturally.

The Periodic Table In 1871, a Russian named Dmitry Mendeleyev arranged the known elements by order of weight, from the lightest to the heaviest. Mendeleyev grouped elements with similar properties into columns. For example, the metals lithium, sodium, and potassium are all in the same column. They all *react*—combine—very easily with other elements. Reactive gases form another column, including fluorine, chlorine, and bromine.

There were some gaps in Mendeleyev's arrangement. He predicted that new elements would be found to fill the gaps. Soon, the predicted elements were found. His basic idea was developed into a table of elements called the *periodic table.* All elements have a place in the periodic table.

Atoms and Elements Some of the ancient Greeks thought the elements were different. They thought this because they knew each one was made from one kind of tiny particle. They called these particles *atoms.* The idea that each element was made from its own kind of atom was forgotten for a while. Then, in 1803, the chemist John Dalton stated that the elements were indeed made up of tiny atoms. Not all chemists believed that atoms existed. Still, they found this idea helped them understand how chemicals combine. It was not until 1905 that Albert Einstein proved that atoms really existed. (*See* **Einstein, Albert.**)

Scientists continued to study atoms. They learned that atoms are very tiny, but they are made from even smaller particles—protons, neutrons, and electrons. The number of protons in an atom determines what element it is. Hydrogen has 1 proton, helium has 2, carbon has 6, and uranium has 92. The number of protons is called the *atomic number* of the element.

Normally, each atom has the same number of electrons as protons. The electrons determine the chemical properties of the element. Sometimes an electron is knocked out of an atom or one is added to the atom. Such an atom, called an *ion,* or an *ionized*

metals

THE PERIODIC TABLE

The periodic table shows the elements in order of their *atomic number.* This number tells how many protons that element has in one of its atoms.

Key:
- Hydrogen — name of element
- H — chemical symbol
- 1 — atomic number

Hydrogen H 1								
Lithium Li 3	Beryllium Be 4							
Sodium Na 11	Magnesium Mg 12							
Potassium K 19	Calcium Ca 20	Scandium Sc 21	Titanium Ti 22	Vanadium V 23	Chromium Cr 24	Manganese Mn 25	Iron Fe 26	Cobalt Co 27
Rubidium Rb 37	Strontium Sr 38	Yttrium Y 39	Zirconium Zr 40	Niobium Nb 41	Molybdenum Mo 42	Technetium Tc 43	Ruthenium Ru 44	Rhodium Rh 45
Cesium Cs 55	Barium Ba 56		Hafnium Hf 72	Tantalum Ta 73	Tungsten W 74	Rhenium Re 75	Osmium Os 76	Iridium Ir 77
Francium Fr 87	Radium Ra 88		104	105	106			

rare earth elements

Lanthanum La 57	Cerium Ce 58	Praseodymium Pr 59	Neodymium Nd 60	Promethium Pm 61	Samarium Sm 62	Europium Eu 63
Actinium Ac 89	Thorium Th 90	Protactinium Pa 91	Uranium U 92	Neptunium Np 93	Plutonium Pu 94	Americium Am 95

atom, does not last very long. The ion attracts another electron or loses the extra one. In atoms that have not been ionized, the electric charge of the protons exactly balances the electric charge of the electrons.

Neutrons do not change one element into another, but they change the weight of the atoms in the element. Carbon, for example, can have 6, 7, or 8 neutrons. The weight of the carbon atom almost equals the number of protons (6) plus the number of neutrons. (*See* **atom.**)

Finding Elements Most elements are found in compounds. In the earth, only gold, silver, carbon, and copper are commonly found as *free*—separate—elements.

It was not easy for early chemists to see how to separate one element from another. They tried to separate the elements in air by putting small animals or burning candles in closed containers of air. This used up most of the oxygen, but produced carbon dioxide. Later, chemists used chemical reactions that would take oxygen from air. What was left

noble
gases

					Helium He 2

nonmetals					

Boron B 5	Carbon C 6	Nitrogen N 7	Oxygen O 8	Fluorine F 9	Neon Ne 10
Aluminum Al 13	Silicon Si 14	Phosphorus P 15	Sulfur S 16	Chlorine Cl 17	Argon Ar 18

Nickel Ni 28	Copper Cu 29	Zinc Zn 30	Gallium Ga 31	Germanium Ge 32	Arsenic As 33	Selenium Se 34	Bromine Br 35	Krypton Kr 36
Palladium Pd 46	Silver Ag 47	Cadmium Cd 48	Indium In 49	Tin Sn 50	Antimony Sb 51	Tellurium Te 52	Iodine I 53	Xenon Xe 54
Platinum Pt 78	Gold Au 79	Mercury Hg 80	Thallium Tl 81	Lead Pb 82	Bismuth Bi 83	Polonium Po 84	Astatine At 85	Radon Rn 86

Gadolinium Gd 64	Terbium Tb 65	Dysprosium Dy 66	Holmium Ho 67	Erbium Er 68	Thulium Tm 69	Ytterbium Yb 70	Lutetium Lu 71
Curium Cm 96	Berkelium Bk 97	Californium Cf 98	Einsteinium Es 99	Fermium Fm 100	Mendelevium Md 101	Nobelium No 102	Lawrencium Lr 103

was mostly nitrogen. Other chemical reactions could be used to remove the nitrogen. Then small amounts of the elements argon, krypton, and xenon were left.

An easy way to get elements from compounds is called *electrolysis*. A strong electric current is put through the compound. One part of the compound collects where the electricity enters. The other part collects where the electricity leaves the compound. Electrolysis can separate water into the two elements it contains—hydrogen and oxygen.

Through electrolysis, it was discovered that salt is a compound. Salt is made from the atoms of two elements.

Abundance of Elements In the universe and solar system, the most abundant elements are hydrogen and helium. On Earth, the most abundant element is iron. But most of the iron is near the center of the planet. The outer layer of the earth is made mostly of oxygen and silicon. Air contains large amounts of nitrogen and oxygen.

See also **molecule.**

elephant

Elephants are the largest animals that live on land, though not the tallest. The giraffe is taller. The biggest elephants may be almost 3.5 meters (11 feet) tall and weigh 5,400 kilograms (12,000 pounds). Elephants have four thick legs to support all this weight.

The elephant's size and long trunk make it easy to recognize. The trunk is really a long upper lip and nose with the nostrils at the tip. The trunk is very useful for smelling, picking up food, and carrying food to the mouth. It also allows the elephant to drink without kneeling. The trunk sucks up the water and either carries it to the mouth or sprays it over the body. Elephants give themselves lots of these showers. They also like to bathe. The water cools them and washes off insect pests.

Most elephants have two *tusks*—long, curved teeth that extend forward on either side of the trunk. Elephants use their tusks as weapons and to dig for food. Their favorite foods are berries, bamboo, sugarcane, coconuts, corn, dates, and plums. They will also eat the bark, leaves, and roots of trees and shrubs.

Elephants that live in open grasslands in Africa have huge ears. When the ears are spread out to the sides, they can pick up the slightest sounds. The animal also uses its ears as fans to keep itself cool. Elephants that live in forests have smaller ears. Shady forests are not as hot as grasslands.

Most elephants live in groups called *herds.* A female usually gives birth to one baby at a time. The baby weighs about 90 kilograms (200 pounds) and is about 90 centimeters (3 feet) high. It can walk soon after birth. The mother feeds and protects her baby. If she sees a lion or other enemy, she may pick the baby up with her trunk. The baby will be an adult when it is 10 to 15 years old. Its life span is 60 to 65 years.

There are two kinds of elephants. One kind lives in Africa and the other in Asia. The Asian elephant has much smaller ears and smaller tusks than the African elephant. The female Asian elephant has no tusks at all. The Asian elephant has one flap, called a *finger,* on the upper tip of its trunk. The African elephant has two "fingers," one above and one below the nostrils.

Asian elephants are much gentler than African elephants. People have trained Asian elephants to carry heavy loads and to do tricks. Though Asian elephants are popular attractions at zoos and circuses, they are endangered in the wild.

Asian elephants have smaller ears and shorter tusks than African elephants.

Asian elephant

African elephant

elevator

When we think of elevators, we usually think of tall buildings. But elevators were used long before the first skyscraper was built. In fact, elevators made skyscrapers possible.

In the early 1800s, elevators were used in deep mines to carry miners, tools, and ore. These elevators had steam engines and cables to raise and lower them. But their steam engines sometimes exploded. Their cables sometimes snapped, causing the elevators to drop hundreds of feet.

Elisha Graves Otis invented the first safety elevator. He became famous when he demonstrated it in 1854. It had a safer steam engine, and a spring-operated safety catch that stopped the elevator if it began to fall too quickly. In 1857, Otis installed the first passenger elevator in a five-story department store in New York City.

By the 1870s, steam-operated elevators were being replaced by hydraulic elevators, which worked by water pressure. An underground tank was filled with water. When more water was pumped into the tank, it pushed the elevator up. When water was let out, the elevator came down.

The hydraulic elevator worked very smoothly, but it had one problem. The underground tank had to be as deep as the building was tall. This was not practical for tall buildings. But hydraulic elevators that use oil instead of water are still used to carry heavy loads short distances. They are used in theaters, for example, to raise and lower sections of the stage. Service stations also use them to lift cars.

In the 1890s, electric motors were built to run elevators in tall buildings and deep mines. Today, almost all elevators are electric. Heavy metal cables are attached to the top of the elevator. The cables go over a pulley that is turned by the motor. The other ends of the cables are attached to a weight, called a *counterweight*. The counterweight is about as heavy as the elevator itself is.

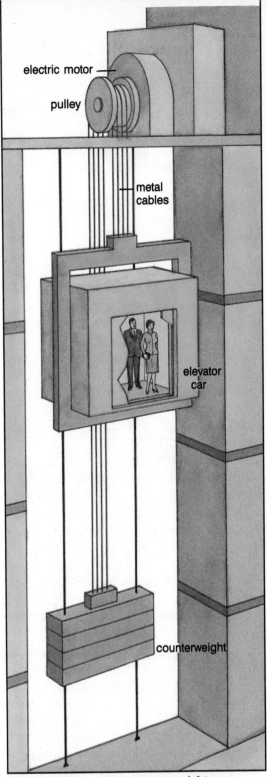

The elevator car and counterweight are balanced. When one goes down, one goes up.

As the motor and pulleys pull the elevator up, the counterweight helps by pulling down on the other end. When the elevator is on the top floor, the counterweight is at the bottom floor.

51

Today, there are about 400,000 passenger elevators in the United States. They travel almost 2 billion miles, up and down, each year. Some move as fast as 20 miles (32 kilometers) per hour. Each day, elevators carry as many passengers as do cars, trains, or aircraft. It would be hard to imagine modern cities without elevators.

Elizabeth I

Elizabeth was a great queen of England during the 1500s. She is called Elizabeth I—Elizabeth the First—because the woman who is the queen of England today is also named Elizabeth—Elizabeth II.

Elizabeth was the daughter of King Henry VIII. She lived in difficult times. England was threatened by bigger, stronger countries, especially Spain. Young Elizabeth's own life was often in danger because other people wanted to rule England.

Elizabeth became queen in 1558, when she was 25 years old. Her intelligence and strong will helped her govern wisely. She worked out a plan to calm bad feeling between Protestants and Catholics. She also challenged Spain and won.

Elizabeth encouraged sea captains like Sir Francis Drake to seize Spanish gold. This enraged the king of Spain. In 1588, he sent a giant fleet of ships, called the Spanish Armada, to invade England.

Elizabeth inspired her troops with her own courage and determination. The English not only stopped the Spanish from invading but also sent the Spanish ships limping home. Events like these gave the English people a new sense of pride.

Elizabeth's long reign of 45 years is often called the Elizabethan Age. England produced some of its greatest literature during this period. The most famous Elizabethan writer was William Shakespeare. (*See* **Shakespeare, William.**)

Elizabeth was an attractive woman with red-gold hair. She loved dancing and horseback riding. Very well educated, she spoke

Elizabeth I was a strong monarch, and most people of England loved her.

Latin, French, Spanish, and Italian. A Frenchman once said, "She is a very great princess, who knows everything."

Elizabeth never married. She was totally dedicated to being a good queen, and she aroused great devotion among her subjects. Late in her life, she said to a group of advisers: "Though God hath raised me high, yet I count this the glory of my crown, that I have reigned with your love."

When Elizabeth died, in 1603, England had become a powerful nation. Its people owed a great deal to the woman they called "Good Queen Bess."

Ellington, Duke

Duke Ellington was a great American composer, bandleader, and pianist. He was one of the most important musicians in the history of jazz music. He wrote more than 1,000 musical works and created new jazz sounds and styles. (*See* **jazz.**)

Edward Kennedy ("Duke") Ellington was born in Washington, D.C., in 1899. He began studying piano when he was 7. In high school, he became interested in jazz. Jazz was a lively new kind of music that bands played at dances and in nightclubs. By the time Ellington was 19, he had his own band.

In 1923 he moved to New York and put together a big jazz band. Early jazz bands had only four to six players. Ellington's had more than 20. He was the band's leader and pianist. The other instruments included a string bass, drums, a banjo, and whole sections of trombones, trumpets, and saxophones. (*See* **musical instrument.**)

Ellington's band became famous at New York's Cotton Club, a nightclub in Harlem. In 1931, the band left New York and went on tour. The big-band sound became very popular in the 1930s, and Duke Ellington's band was one of the best. They traveled throughout the United States, playing at dances and nightclubs. They also made hundreds of recordings. Even people who never saw the band in person knew Duke Ellington's music from his records.

Some musicians stayed with Ellington's band for many years. He knew them so well that he could write music that showed off their special talents. He used the band to create new jazz styles. He liked to combine several different instruments to produce new sound "colors." For example, in a song called "Mood Indigo," a bass clarinet, a trombone, and a trumpet played together.

Early jazz pieces were very short and were almost always played in nightclubs. But the Duke wrote many longer works and played some of them at jazz concerts. His band was the first jazz band to play in famous concert halls, such as Carnegie Hall in New York City. Ellington also wrote music for Broadway shows, operas, ballets, films, and church services.

Some of Ellington's tunes became very famous. Among them are "Satin Doll," "Sophisticated Lady," and "Solitude." Jazz musicians play them even today.

Duke Ellington (at piano) appears with his band during the 1940s.

Ellington never retired. He traveled with his band until the last months of his life. By then, he was famous around the world. He died in 1974.

El Salvador, *see* Central America

encyclopedia

An encyclopedia is a book or a set of books with information about many subjects. You can use an encyclopedia to learn about science, history, languages, foods, toys, and other things. Many people begin their education by reading an encyclopedia.

Most encyclopedias consist of several books, called *volumes.* Articles are usually arranged in alphabetical order, but they may be arranged by subject. Articles are often illustrated with photographs, drawings, maps, or charts. This is done to make information clearer to readers.

Some encyclopedias, like the one you are reading, are *general.* They have information on many subjects. Others are *specialized.* These have information on one subject, such as sports or music.

The ancient Greeks and Romans made the first encyclopedias we know of. They wanted to have all their knowledge in one place. So they collected information from the experts of their time. Centuries later, the Chinese and the Arabs wrote encyclopedias.

After the printing press was invented, people in many European countries printed encyclopedias. Two of the most famous came out in the 1700s. One was the French *Encyclopeédie.* The first of its 28 volumes came out in 1751. Each article was written by an expert. But the articles gave opinions as well as facts. The French government did not like that, so it refused to allow some articles to be printed.

The *Encyclopedia Britannica* was first published in 1771, in Scotland. Later it was published in England. Now it is published in the United States, too. For many years, it was considered the greatest English-language encyclopedia.

Encyclopedias for children did not appear until the 1900s. Adults realized that children wanted information, too, and adult encyclopedias were often too difficult for children to read and understand.

Once an encyclopedia is printed, it gradually becomes out-of-date, because of new events and discoveries. An encyclopedia printed in 1950 has no articles about space travel or home computers. Encyclopedia owners can often purchase a new *yearbook* volume each year to get new information.

Today, people who make encyclopedias use computers to keep up-to-date. In fact, the encyclopedias of the future may be available on computer disks as well as in books. You may soon be able to sit down at your home or library computer and read an up-to-the-minute encyclopedia article.

endangered animals, *see* **animals, endangered**

General encyclopedias like those being used below often have many volumes. Special encyclopedias are about a single subject such as baseball (right).

Before a race, athletes eat foods their bodies can burn for quick energy.
A power company burns oil or gas fuel to make electricity for your home.

energy

When you wake up on a sunny morning and say you feel full of energy, what do you mean? Probably you mean that you feel ready to run, hike, swim, or play games. Sometimes, you may not be so lucky. Your mother may expect you to use all your energy to clean up your room or do other work around the house.

You know what energy feels like. But what exactly is it? Scientists define energy simply as "the ability to do work." In fact, the word *energy* comes from the Greek word *ergon,* meaning "work."

Energy in Science Scientists have many reasons to study energy. They want to know how many different kinds there are, and they want to know how to store it and use it. They are especially interested in ways to change one kind of energy into another. For example, the energy you feel comes from the food you eat. Since the energy comes from chemical changes in the food, we call it *chemical energy.* When you use your energy to move something, you are changing chemical energy into *mechanical energy*—the kind of energy that can lift or move things.

Cars, too, change chemical energy into mechanical energy. When they burn gasoline, chemical changes happen that produce energy. When that energy is used to turn the wheels and move the car, it has become mechanical energy.

Knowing how to change energy into different forms is very important to us. In an electric power plant, we burn a fuel to generate electrical power. We are changing the chemical energy in the fuel to *electrical energy.* Electrical energy can be sent out in electrical wires to factories, offices, and homes, so that many people can use it. (*See* **electric power.**)

In our homes, we change electrical energy into many other forms of energy. When electricity runs a toaster, we are changing electrical energy to *heat energy.* When it lights a light bulb, we are changing electrical energy to *radiant energy.* When it runs a fan, the electricity is moving the blades, so it is being changed to mechanical energy.

Energy from the Sun Where does energy come from? Almost all of the energy we use comes from the sun. The sun is like a giant energy factory. Every second, the earth receives huge amounts of energy from the sun. (*See* **solar energy.**)

55

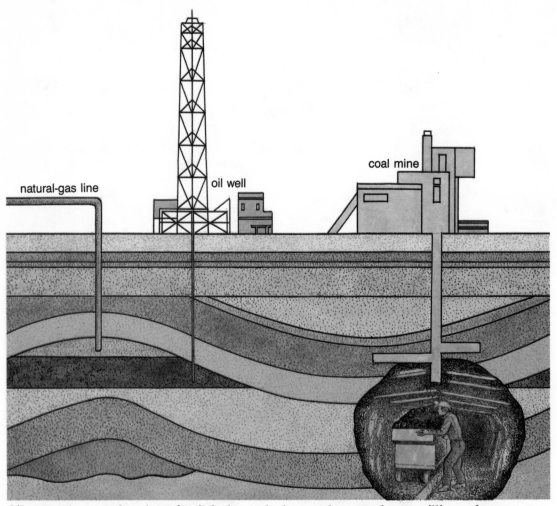

natural-gas line

oil well

coal mine

Oil, natural gas, and coal are fossil fuels, made deep underground over millions of years. They are also *non-renewable*—if they are used up, they cannot be replaced.

The easiest way to get energy from the sun is to use its light. If a building has windows, the sun lights the rooms during the day. The sun also helps heat the building.

Our bodies get all their energy from the sun. Plants can grow only in sunlight. They change some of the sun's energy into food. When we eat plants or animals that have eaten plants, our bodies make energy from the food. (*See* **photosynthesis** and **plant.**)

The sun also produces all the fuels that we burn for energy. Trees need sunlight to grow. Later, we can cut a tree down and burn it for energy. Coal, oil, and gasoline all come from plants that lived millions of years ago. So these fuels were produced by the sun's energy, too. (*See* **petroleum.**)

The sun's energy causes other important things to happen. The warmth of the sun makes water in oceans, lakes, and rivers evaporate into the air. Later, the water falls as rain or snow, and then runs downhill in streams and rivers. For centuries, people have used the energy of this running water to do work. The sun also helps cause the wind. In some parts of the world, people get useful energy from windmills.

Energy from the Earth We get some energy from heat deep inside the earth. For example, in Iceland, people use hot water from deep springs to heat houses and offices. This energy comes from radioactive elements in rocks. These radioactive elements undergo nuclear reactions that produce heat.

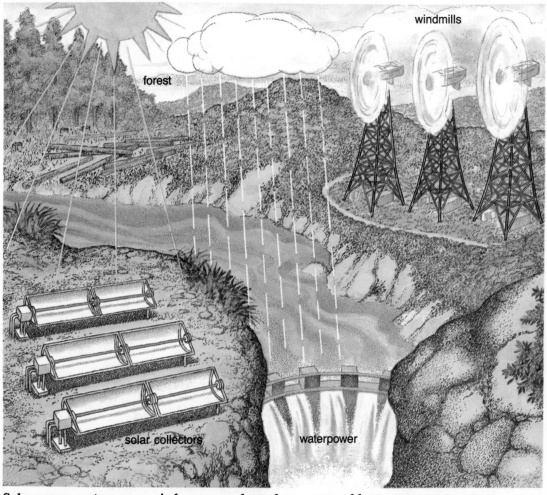

windmills

forest

solar collectors

waterpower

Solar power, waterpower, wind power, and wood are *renewable* energy sources. The sun shines, water falls, wind blows, and trees grow all the time.

People have learned how to cause nuclear reactions themselves. In many parts of the world, there are nuclear power plants that produce electric power. (*See* **nuclear power.**)

Running Out of Energy Coal, oil, and natural gas are *fossil fuels.* They formed in the earth from plants and animals that died millions of years ago. We have huge amounts of these fuels, but our supply is limited.

Scientists think there is enough oil, coal, and natural gas to last for many years. But they may become much more expensive. Car designers are making engines that need less fuel, and people are trying to *conserve* energy—to use only as much as we really need. At the same time, we are looking for other kinds of energy.

Other Sources of Energy A small piece of nuclear fuel can produce tremendous amounts of energy. However, the waste products from a nuclear power plant are very dangerous to living things. In addition, a serious accident in a nuclear plant can scatter poisonous materials across hundreds or thousands of miles. Scientists hope to develop a new, less dangerous way of getting nuclear energy called *fusion.*

Many energy scientists are studying ways to harness the power of the sun and the weather. In desert areas, they are making electricity from sunlight. Along ocean shorelines, they are making electricity from waves. But so far, these new sources provide only a small amount of energy.

History of Energy Use The earliest people had only the energy from the sun for warmth and light, and the energy that their own bodies could take from the food they ate. Then, about 500,000 years ago, humans learned to use fire. They learned that burning wood could keep them warm at night and could be used to cook food.

About 3,000 years ago, people in China found that a gas escaping through cracks in the earth would burn. They learned how to use it for cooking, heating, and lighting. We still use natural gas today for cooking and heating. The Chinese also discovered small amounts of sticky crude oil that would burn.

By the year 1000, the Chinese were also burning coal. When the European Marco Polo wrote about his travels in China in the 1200s, he said the Chinese burned black rocks. Europeans thought he was lying, but soon they discovered coal in Europe, too.

Wood was still the most important fuel. But in some parts of the world, there was not enough of it. There was not much wood in Britain, for example, so people there began to burn coal in their homes sometime in the 1500s.

In the late 1800s, Americans used gas flames to light houses and streets.

In the 1700s, the people of Britain began building factories. Seeking a good way to use energy to run machines, they turned to James Watt's steam engine. The engine burned coal to make steam. Heat from the steam was turned into mechanical energy. Soon, steam engines were powering locomotives on railroads. (*See* **steam engine.**)

Oil first became important when people started to drive cars. Coal-powered engines must be very large. Cars needed a good liquid fuel such as gasoline, which is made from oil. Gasoline engines can be made small enough to fit in the palm of your hand, if need be. Soon, people were searching for oil all over the world. Oil usually is found deep beneath the ground. Engineers have to dig a deep well and pump the oil up.

Energy from falling water is already widely used. Water rushing through dams provides power for many electric plants, but dams can be built only where there are rivers. (*See* **dam** and **waterpower.**)

Other Energy Concerns There are many other problems in the use of energy. For example, when we burn coal, oil, or gasoline, we create smoke and fumes. In some places, the sun helps turn these fumes into choking smog. (*See* **air pollution.**)

Mining coal and drilling for oil can also damage the environment. In some places, coal miners tear up large areas of land to reach coal deposits. In other places, miners must tunnel deep into the earth for coal. Many miners have developed lung problems from breathing coal dust.

Energy is important to the way we live. Governments and scientists in many parts of the world are seeking new sources of energy so that we won't run out of energy. They may find safe ways of making nuclear energy, or they may find new ways to harness the energy of sun, wind, and water. Perhaps some completely new source of energy will be found. After all, 300 years ago, most of the world's people did not even guess that there was oil under the ground.

See also **fuel.**

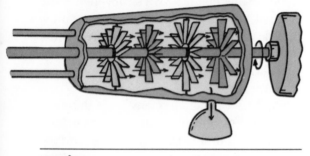

A waterwheel (above) is an early kind of turbine engine. Water in a stream turns the wheel, providing energy.
A steam turbine (below) helps generate electricity. Steam forced into the turbine from pipes on the left causes the drive shaft to turn. The drive shaft is connected to a generator, which makes electricity.

engine

The Indianapolis 500 is America's oldest car race. The race begins every year with a traditional announcement to drivers: "Gentlemen, start your engines!"

A thunderous roar goes up as all the race-cars' engines start together. Soon, those engines are powering the cars to speeds of over 200 miles per hour.

The engines at the Indianapolis 500 are among the most powerful car engines in the world. Yet they work in basically the same way as the engine in a family car.

Car engines are *internal-combustion* engines. *Internal* means "inside," and *combustion* means "burning." The internal-combustion engine gets its power by burning a fuel inside the engine.

What Is an Engine? Basically, an engine is any device that puts mechanical energy to work. Most engines get their energy from a fuel that is burned. The heat from burning fuel becomes mechanical energy that starts the engine in motion and keeps it running. (*See* **energy**.)

Automobile engines are just a few of the many engines that provide power for the modern world. Engines are the driving force in many forms of transportation. Jet planes are powered by engines. Many trains are powered by electric engines. Trucks and buses run on engines much like those in cars.

Electric power plants also depend on a kind of engine called a *turbine*. These engines start the process that sends electricity to your home. Engines do much of the work in factories. You probably have many smaller engines in your home. Smaller engines are usually called *motors*. Motors in your home drive fans, air conditioners, vacuum cleaners, refrigerators, dishwashers, and other machines.

History of Engines The first engines were *turbines* of one kind or another. A turbine is a fan that is turned by a moving fluid.

The most useful early turbines were powered by running water. Water running in a stream turned a simple kind of turbine called a *waterwheel*. The wheel then turned other machinery, such as millstones. Millstones are heavy wheels used to grind grain, such as wheat, into flour.

In windy areas, windmills were used as turbines. The wind pushing against large sails started machinery turning. Windmills were often used to pump water from wells.

Today, turbines are still important. Large turbines are used in nearly all electric power plants. Another kind of turbine powers a jet airplane. Modern turbine engines are more complicated than waterwheels or windmills. In electric power plants, the pressure—the pushing force—comes from steam. In jet engines, the pressure comes from an expanding gas produced by burning fuel.

No one is sure exactly when waterwheels and windmills were invented. The ancient Egyptians and Sumerians used them. Eventually, they were replaced by steam engines.

Today, people still use waterwheels and windmills to run generators that produce electric power.

The Steam Engine In the late 1600s, people began to invent engines that got their power from burning fuel. Inventors knew that water heated beyond the boiling point turns to steam, and that the steam causes a lot of pressure. They were sure that this pressure could do mechanical work.

The first steam engines did not work very well. Lots of steam was allowed to escape, which lowered the pressure. That meant a lot of fuel—usually wood—was wasted in order to heat water to make steam.

In the 1780s, James Watt developed a better steam engine. He found ways to control the steam pressure. This made his engine more powerful, and wasted less fuel.

Watt's steam engine soon changed the world. Steam engines made railroad trains possible. They made factories more productive. Before steam engines, most factory work was done by hand. (*See* **steam engine.**)

Some inventors hoped that a steam engine could run a carriage that a person could drive alone—an automobile. The Stanley Steamer was a steam-driven automobile. It was powerful and fast, but it was also very heavy and it used lots of fuel. Steam engines had to be big and heavy. It was also dangerous. If steam pressure got too high, the engine could explode.

The Internal-Combustion Engine In the late 1800s, inventors started trying to make smaller, safer engines. In a steam engine, the fire that heats the water to produce steam is outside the engine. But the inventors wanted the fire to be *internal* — inside the engine—where it could create mechanical energy directly.

Nikolaus Otto of Germany built the most successful of the early internal combustion engines. His first small engine was powered by the kind of gas used for lighting. He then made a better one that ran on gasoline. In

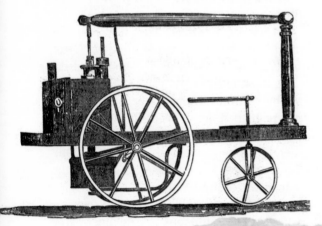

James Watt, inventor of the first practical steam engine, hoped the engine would provide power for a locomotive like the one at left. By 1900, there were thousands of steam locomotives like the one below.

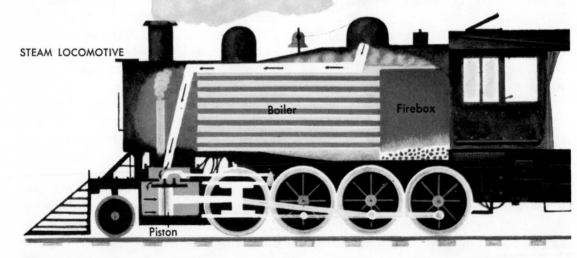

STEAM LOCOMOTIVE

Boiler

Firebox

Piston

1885, another German inventor, Karl Benz, built the first automobile powered by a gasoline engine. Today's car engines work much like those built by Otto and Benz.

Let's look first at how an internal-combustion engine works. What happens when you turn the key in a car's ignition to start?

The process begins in the fuel system. Gasoline from the car's gas tank goes to a device called the *carburetor.* The carburetor mixes a small amount of fuel with air.

The air-fuel mixture is then sent to the *cylinders.* The round, hollow cylinders are like short pieces of pipe closed at one end. Inside each cylinder is a *piston.* The piston is a metal piece that moves up and down inside the cylinder.

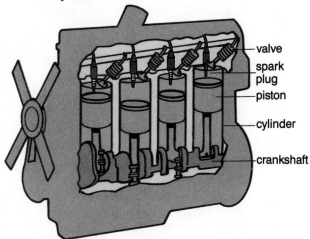

valve
spark plug
piston
cylinder
crankshaft

Inside the cylinder, the air-fuel mixture is ignited—lit—by an electrical spark from a *spark plug.* The spark plug gets its electricity from the car's battery.

When the air-fuel mixture is ignited, a small explosion takes place in the cylinder. That explosion forces the piston to move in the cylinder.

Most car engines have at least four cylinders. Many have six or eight. The pistons in an engine work together. In a four-cylinder car, there are always two pistons going up while two are going down.

The pistons are connected to the car's crank shaft. Their up-and-down motion turns the crank shaft. The crank shaft is connected to the drive shaft, which makes the wheels turn.

All of that activity in a car's engine happens very fast. The pistons may go up and down more than 1,000 times every minute. It depends on how fast you are driving. That fast movement can make a car's engine very hot. That is why engines have cooling systems. The cooling system keeps water or another coolant moving around the engine to keep it from overheating. (*See* **automobile.**)

Below, a cylinder in a gasoline engine.
1. Fuel and air enter a cylinder.
2. The spark plug ignites the mixture.
3. The explosion drives the piston down.
4. The piston pushes exhaust gases out.
Left, a car engine with four cylinders.

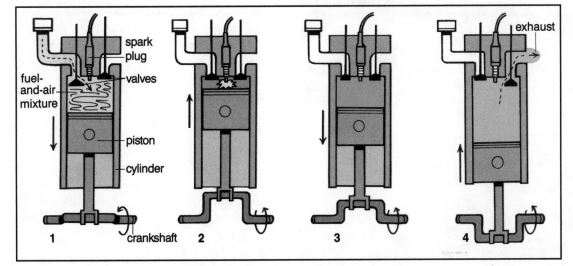

spark plug
valves
fuel-and-air mixture
piston
cylinder
crankshaft
exhaust
1
2
3
4

Other Kinds of Engines A diesel engine works in very much the same way as a gasoline engine. But the fuel is not ignited inside the cylinder by a spark. Instead, pressure in the cylinder causes the air to heat up, igniting the fuel.

Engines powered by electricity are used to run some trains and factory machinery. Electric motors are also used in many small appliances. (*See* **electric motor.**)

Many people consider rockets to be engines. A rocket is propelled forward as gases heated by the burning of the rocket's fuel are released backward. (*See* **rocket.**)

See also **jet engine** and **wind power.**

England, *see* United Kingdom

English history

England is the main part of a country called the United Kingdom. If you want to read about the country's geography and its people today, *see* **United Kingdom.**

England is small, but it has a long and interesting history. At one time, people from England ruled lands all over the world. It is because of English energy and boldness that

Prince Charles may become king of England after his mother, Elizabeth II.

you speak English and the book you are holding is written in English.

Early Times Long ago, the people of England lived very simply, by hunting. They had no writing, so little is known about them. One thing we do know is that some of them built big structures out of stone, maybe for religious purposes. The best known of these structures is Stonehenge. (*See* **Stonehenge.**)

Then, about 600 B.C., invaders from Europe arrived. They were called Celts, and they gradually settled throughout the islands of Britain and Ireland. When other peoples invaded the islands, they pushed the Celts to the west and north. Today, descendants of the Celts live in Wales and Cornwall, in parts of Scotland, on the Isle of Man in the Irish Sea, and across the Irish Sea in Ireland. Some people in these areas continue to speak Celtic languages. (*See* **Celts.**)

Around the time of Christ, the Romans built a strong empire. It centered on the Mediterranean Sea but also spread into northern Europe. The Romans invaded England in 54 B.C., and conquered it a few years later. They stayed in England for about 400 years. They built forts, roads, walls, and towns. The city of London began as the Roman town of Londinium.

The Roman Empire began to crumble in the 400s, and Roman soldiers in England were called home to defend Italy. With the Roman soldiers gone, other invaders soon started attacking England from northern Europe. These were the Angles, Saxons, and Jutes. After they settled in England, they became known as Anglo-Saxons. The name *England* comes from the name *Angle-land.* (*See* **Anglo-Saxons.**)

The Anglo-Saxons formed many small kingdoms that often fought each other. This made it easier for the Danes to invade England, beginning in the 800s. One Anglo-Saxon king, Alfred the Great, was able to force the Danes to live only in certain areas of England. But he could not get them out of the country entirely.

Stonehenge

Vikings

Tower of London

Roman Conquest

Norman Conquest

Lord Nelson

Spanish Armada

Elizabeth I

Battle of Trafalgar

Houses of Parliament

Victoria

Churchill

St. Paul's Cathedral

Elizabeth II

Change and Growth Across the Channel from England lies the French region known as Normandy. A strong Norman leader named William thought that he should be king of England. He was related to its Anglo-Saxon ruler and said he had been promised the crown. So he invaded England in 1066 and defeated the English at the Battle of Hastings. This Norman conquest gave William his title—William the Conqueror.

The Normans brought many changes to England. William gave land to his nobles. In return, they owed him military service and money. This system, called *feudalism,* gave the king more power than the Anglo-Saxon rulers had ever had. (*See* **Middle Ages.**)

After William the Conqueror, most of the kings of England made the English government stronger. For example, they set up courts to handle legal disputes. This added to royal power. People who wanted justice had to go to a representative of the king instead of settling the case among themselves. As time went on, the decisions of earlier judges were used as guides by later judges. This system of law, called *common law,* is the basis for law in the United States and several other countries.

The nobles sometimes objected to actions by the king. One ruler, King John, was very

Factories made England rich, but the early factories were often miserable, unhealthy places to work.

King Henry VIII was a strong king who helped make England a powerful nation.

unpopular because he increased taxes. In the year 1215, a group of nobles forced him to sign a document called Magna Carta—the Great Charter. It put some limits on royal power. (*See* **Magna Carta.**)

Another important event of the 1200s was the growth of Parliament—a group of nobles and others who advised the king and helped rule England.

England did not develop without warfare. Beginning in the early 1330s, the English struggled with the French over who should rule various areas of France. By the time this Hundred Years' War was over, the French controlled almost all of their own land.

At home, two families, the House of Lancaster and the House of York, struggled over who should rule England. This civil war raged on and off for almost 100 years. Finally, in 1485, Henry Tudor of the House of Lancaster defeated the Yorkists at Bosworth Field. He married Elizabeth of York and ruled as Henry VII.

Kings and Parliament By the 1500s, England's capital, London, was a bustling city of almost 200,000 people. Foreign trade brought wealth, which was used to build beautiful churches and fine homes. England also had two fine universities, Oxford and Cambridge.

This was a time of religious conflict, however. A movement called the Reformation

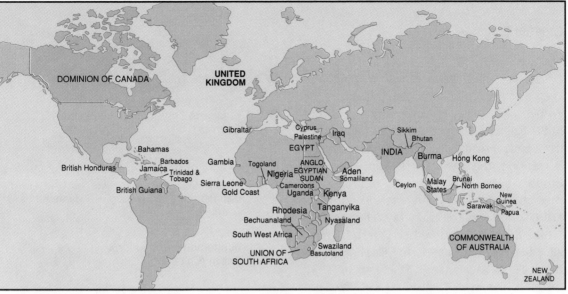

Because Britain had colonies around the globe, it was said that the sun never set on the British Empire. Most of the British colonies have become independent countries. Yet many still have special ties of friendship with Britian.

was changing Christianity. In England, King Henry VIII broke away from the Catholic Church and set up a separate Church of England. (*See* **Reformation.**)

Henry's daughter, Queen Elizabeth I, kept peace among religious groups. During her reign, England defeated the invading Spanish Armada and became a world power. Elizabeth also sent explorers to North America, where England soon set up colonies. (*See* **Elizabeth I.**)

Religious conflict broke out again in the 1600s. Some people were dissatisfied with the Church of England. They were called Puritans. Many migrated to America, but those who stayed in England were soon fighting a bloody civil war. The Puritans wanted Parliament alone to rule England. They captured King Charles I and executed him. A Puritan leader named Oliver Cromwell became England's ruler. But after he died, the son of Charles I became King Charles II.

Since the late 1600s, there has always been a king or queen of England. But they have gradually become less powerful. Laws were passed to limit what the king or queen could do. More and more ordinary people gained the right to vote.

Parliament is now the real ruler of England. It controls the country through the election of a *prime minister,* who represents the voters. Today, England has a *democratic* government—the people make the most important decisions. The king or queen is a symbol of the nation's past and the ideas its people value.

Factories and Empire In the 1700s, a series of changes began in England that eventually spread over the whole world. People started to make goods by machine in factories instead of making them by hand at home. This way of doing things led to many other changes, known as the Industrial Revolution. The Industrial Revolution turned England into a mighty workshop. The English mined coal, made steel, and sold thousands of their products abroad. (*See* **Industrial Revolution.**)

England was also becoming the center of a great empire. The Act of Union of 1707 had joined England, Scotland, and Wales to form the United Kingdom, also called Great Britain. Ireland was made part of the United Kingdom in 1800. The Scots, Welsh, and Irish did much to make England the strongest country in the world.

England lost some of its North American colonies when the United States became independent. But the English controlled many other lands. These included Canada, islands in the Caribbean Sea, India, Australia, New Zealand, and colonies in Africa. English customs, the English language, and English law spread all over the world.

England often went to war to gain and keep power. The English fought the French—and won—in North America and in India. England also struggled to keep France from conquering Europe during the French Revolution and the rule of Napoleon. The English owed much to their navy and to their military leaders, such as Viscount Horatio Nelson and the Duke of Wellington.

Like Elizabeth I before her, Queen Victoria gave her name to a period of English greatness. The Victorian Age lasted from 1837 through the rest of the 1800s. England gained tremendous wealth and power during Victoria's reign.

The 1900s England lost much of its power during the 1900s. It fought with France against Germany and Austria in World War I. Although England was on the winning side, almost a million English people lost their lives. (*See* **World War I.**)

England also lost some of the wealth it had gained through manufacturing and trade. The United States—with many more people and resources—took England's place as the most important industrial nation.

World War II was hard on the English. At one time, in 1940 and 1941, England was the only country fighting Germany. Night after night, the Germans bombed London and other centers. The prime minister, Sir Winston Churchill, led the English to victory in what he called their "finest hour." (*See* **Churchill, Sir Winston** and **World War II.**)

Beginning in the 1950s, most of the colonies England had ruled gained their independence. Canada and Australia are still linked to England through an organization called the Commonwealth of Nations. But the ties are those only of friendship.

England is still an important nation. People love the land for its beauty. They admire English literature and learning. And all democratic governments owe a great deal to English traditions of justice.

See also **English language; English writers; Drake, Sir Francis;** and **Raleigh, Sir Walter.**

el lagarto ("the lizard") → **alligator**
Spanish

dachshund ("badger dog") → **dachshund**
German

achitomon → **chipmunk**
Indian (Chippewa)

These three animal names came into English from other languages.

English language

The English language is the language you are now reading. More than 400 million people in the world speak English as their first language. Millions more learn English as a second language for business, education, travel, and communication. English is the language of the United States, most of Canada, the British Isles, Australia, New Zealand, South Africa, many islands in the Caribbean and the Pacific, and Guyana in South America. In many other countries, such as India and some countries in Africa, English is one of several official languages.

English has more than a half-million words, far more than any other language. Yet it keeps growing. New words come in with new inventions. With computers came *byte* and a new meaning for *bit*. Space travel gave us *countdown, astronaut,* and a new meaning for *launch.*

English also adopts many of its words from other languages. Recently, Spanish-speaking immigrants to the United States brought us *barrio* ("neighborhood") and *bodega* ("grocery store"). *Parka* is one of the words that came from the Eskimo people of Alaska. The American Indians gave English many words, including *chipmunk*. English has borrowed and kept words from other languages as well.

How English Developed The English language started around the year 450. Germanic peoples—the Angles, Saxons, and Jutes—invaded Britain and settled there. In England, their languages mixed, and became the language we call *Old English* or *Anglo-Saxon*. Afterward, the language kept growing and changing. But many Old English words—such as *lamb, bread, love,* and *earth*—are still part of English.

In 597, Christianity came to England, bringing Latin words. The Latin words *angelus* and *candela* became *angel* and *candle*. Then people from Scandinavia invaded, and new words like *sky, leg,* and *skull* came with them. In different parts of England, people used different words and pronunciations. But by the year 900, *the King's English*—English as spoken by the rulers—was considered the best English.

A great change came in 1066. That was when the Normans, from France, conquered England. Many people continued to speak English, but French became the official language of government and business. Many French words came into the English language. By 1100, the language was so different that people today call it by a different name—*Middle English*. The Normans in England gradually blended with the Anglo-Saxons, but their words remained. Words like *castle, mutton,* and *royal* have come from Norman French.

Later, London's English was considered the best. By 1500, the language had again changed so much that it is known today as *Modern English*. Modern English is the English you speak and read today. But the earliest Modern English is not easy for us to read now. Shakespeare, for example, wrote in Modern English. Yet the way his characters speak in his plays may sound very unusual to us.

Just before Shakespeare was born, England began to explore the world. England set up colonies in America, India, Australia, and Africa. People in these lands began to speak English. The language once spoken by

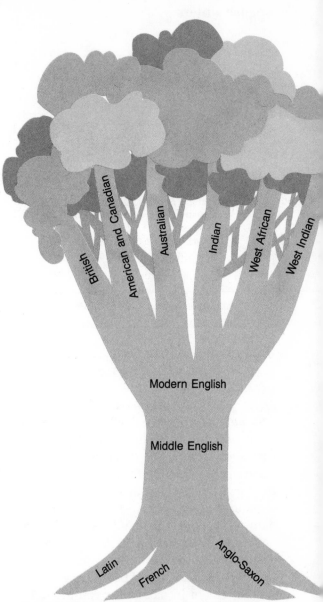

English began as the language of a small group of tribes. After many changes, it has become a language spoken around the world.

a few thousand Germanic settlers was starting to become a world language.

Spelling, Pronunciation, and Vocabulary For many hundreds of years, people spelled words the way they sounded. Once printing presses were invented, printers tried to keep spellings from changing, to make their job easier. So pronunciations changed while many spellings stayed the same. For example, people used to pronounce the *gh* in *night*, the *k* in *know*, and the *l* in *walk*. We still use these spellings, even though we pronounce the words differently.

67

English can be different!	
When Americans say:	**The British say:**
apartment	flat
cookie	biscuit
dessert	sweet
elevator	lift
French fries	chips
garbage can	dust bin
gasoline	petrol
potato chips	crisps
sidewalk	pavement
sweater	jumper
truck	lorry
trunk (of a car)	boot
underpass	subway
washcloth	face flannel

People in America speak American English. Sometimes, the American word for a thing is different from the word used in England. Americans say *elevator* (not *lift*), and *railroad* (not *railway*). Spellings may be different, too. Americans use the spellings *color* (not *colour*), and *center* (not *centre*). Canada, Australia, and South Africa have some of their own words, pronunciations, and spellings. In countries where English is one of many languages, the country's own words and ways of saying things become part of written and spoken English.

British English used to be the only form of English taught in most other countries. Today, many people learn American English instead. All forms of English are basically the same, despite differences from place to place. All English-speaking people can read each other's English, even though we may say words differently. This helps us continue to share the language.

English writers

Many centuries ago, nearly everyone who spoke English lived in the country of England (now a part of the United Kingdom). Writers in England produced many stories, poems, and plays that people all over the world still enjoy.

Early English Writers People in England were writing in English before the year 1000. Some of them wrote down stories that people had been telling for many years—stories about heroes, villains, and monsters.

One of these tales was called *Beowulf.* It tells how the hero Beowulf fought and killed a man-eating monster named Grendel. At the end of the story, Beowulf fights a dragon and kills it, but soon dies of his wounds.

Many years later, in the 1300s, a great poet named Geoffrey Chaucer wrote story poems in English. His most famous book, *The Canterbury Tales,* is about a group of travelers who are walking to the English city of Canterbury to visit a great cathedral. To pass the time, they begin telling each other stories. Some of the stories are funny, some are sad, and some tell of great adventures. We still enjoy reading Chaucer today, even though the English he used now seems very strange and old-fashioned.

Canterbury Tales

At nyght was come into that hostelrye
Wele nyne and twenty in a compaignie,
Of sondry folk, by aventure yfalle
In felaweshipe, and pilgrimes were
     they alle,
That toward Caunterbury wolden ryde.

Shakespeare The greatest of all English writers lived 300 years after Chaucer. William Shakespeare was an actor and a writer of many different kinds of plays. One of his most popular plays is the tragedy *Macbeth.* It is about a nobleman who murders a king so he can become king himself. Shakespeare died in 1616, a few years before the first people from England came to America. (*See* **Shakespeare, William.**)

Novelists In the 1700s and 1800s, some writers in England began to write long stories called *novels.* Novels were printed in books, and people bought them to read for pleasure.

Many novels told of exciting adventures. Sir Walter Scott's *Ivanhoe* is about a young man's adventures during the time of Robin Hood. Other novels told stories about love or simply about life at that time. For example, Jane Austen's heroines do not travel very far from home. But *Pride and Prejudice* and her other books tell a lot about human nature

Macbeth

Macbeth: I have done the deed. Didst thou
    not hear a noise?
Lady Macbeth: I heard the owl scream and
    the crickets cry.
    Did you not speak?
Macbeth: When?
Lady Macbeth: Now.
Macbeth: As I descended?
Lady Macbeth: Aye.

and the difference between good actions and bad actions.

One of the great writers of novels was Charles Dickens. In *David Copperfield,* he told about a poor young boy growing up in England in the 1800s. David Copperfield's childhood was something like Dickens' own childhood. In a shorter story called "A Christmas Carol," Dickens wrote about a coldhearted businessman named Scrooge who finally discovered the meaning of Christmas. The story has been retold over the years in movies and plays.

Poetry Some of the most famous English writers wrote poetry. John Milton was a government official in the 1600s who wrote a long poem based on the biblical story of Adam and Eve. It was called *Paradise Lost.* Some people think it is the greatest long poem in English.

Beginning about 1800, a group of English poets began writing beautiful poems about nature and about their own deepest longings. William Wordsworth and Percy Bysshe Shelley were two of these Romantic poets.

Other Writers Many English writers wrote about important people and events. Jonathan Swift wrote essays that poked fun at evil men and made them seem ridiculous. This kind of writing is called *satire.*

Samuel Johnson prepared the first great dictionary of the English language. Most later dictionaries in England and America were based on his work. After he died, his friend James Boswell wrote *The Life of Samuel Johnson.* This was the first great *biography*—book telling about a person's life.

Some writers were political leaders. Edmund Burke wrote great speeches in the 1700s. One was about Britain and its American colonies. Burke believed that Britain should let the colonies be independent.

In the 1900s, Sir Winston Churchill was prime minister of Britain. His speeches encouraged the British to keep fighting during World War II. Churchill also wrote novels and books about history. (*See* **Churchill, Sir Winston.**)

Writing Outside England Beginning in the 1700s, many people began writing in English while living in countries other than England. Robert Burns, a Scottish poet, wrote poems about Scottish life. In these poems, he used the speech patterns heard in Scotland. In America, poetry, speeches, and essays were being written, especially once Americans began to argue that America should be free. (*See* **American writers.**)

At the end of the 1800s, Rudyard Kipling, an Englishman in India, wrote poems and stories blending Indian and English ideas. He is most famous for *The Jungle Book*.

In the early 1900s, many of the best writers in English were Irish, such as William Butler Yeats, a poet, and James Joyce, a novelist. Joyce wrote books that made us think about how the words we use to describe life change the way we see things.

See also **English language** and **children's books.**

---

environment

The environment is everything around us. It includes all living things. It also includes everything that is not alive, such as the soil, the air, and the water at a particular place.

Balance in Nature In a healthy environment, the living things have adjusted to each other and to the conditions in that environment. We call this a *balanced* environment. Such an environment can often stay the same for hundreds of years.

Sometimes, however, a balanced environment may become unbalanced. A disease may wipe out one group of living things. Climate may change. A hurricane or forest fire may change the environment. It may take many, many years for the environment to become balanced again.

Often, people are responsible for disturbing the balance of nature. For example, farmers may kill hawks that eat their farm animals. But hawks eat more than just chickens. In fact, hawks eat many field mice and just a few chickens. When you get rid of the hawks, you destroy the balance. Although the chickens are protected, now there are too many field mice. They may cause more damage than the hawks ever did.

Nature can get out of balance in other ways as well. The suburbs outside cities provide an excellent environment for white-tailed deer. They thrive in the wooded hills and open fields. The deer do not have to be wary of hunters, because hunting is usually

This forest was killed by acid rain—a poison created by chemical wastes in the air. Acid rain damages plants and also kills fish and other wildlife.

Aluminum cans are melted down and made into new cans at this recycling plant.

illegal in suburbs. There are too many people and too many houses to allow guns to be fired. As a result, many suburbs now have too many deer. They eat shrubs, vegetable gardens, flowers, and fruit trees. They are a hazard to drivers. Some of these animals carry ticks that can cause disease.

Like the animal community, the plant community can become unbalanced. Fertilizer helps crops grow. But sometimes rain washes the fertilizer away, into lakes and rivers. The fertilizer makes tiny algae grow out of control. They may completely cover a lake. When the food runs out, the algae die. Bacteria break down the dead algae. The lake begins to smell, and animals in the lake may die, too.

Water pollution kills plants and animals and endangers the human water supply.

Poisons in the Environment Human activities can make the environment unhealthy. The gasoline burned inside car engines produces gases that poison the air. Factories burn fuels to run machines, and these burning fuels, too, put poisons into the air. (*See* **air pollution.**)

Human activities also poison water. Some factories produce liquid wastes that run into rivers. Often, these wastes contain poisons. (*See* **water pollution.**)

Sometimes, useful chemicals cause problems in the environment. DDT is a poison that once was used in the United States to kill insects. It did control insects, but the DDT harmed other animals as well, by traveling up the *food chain.* The food chain is the order in which animals prey on each other. Small animals eat insects. Larger animals eat the smaller animals. The large animals are eaten by still larger animals, including people. (*See* **food chain.**)

When small animals ate the poisoned insects, they took in the DDT, too. The animals stored the DDT in their cells. When larger animals ate these small animals, the DDT was passed on to the larger animals. Living things low on the food chain had only a little DDT. Living things high on the food chain had a lot of DDT in their bodies.

Eagles are high on the food chain. They started laying eggs with thin, soft shells. The shells cracked too soon, and the baby birds did not hatch.

Scientists studying birds noticed that eagles were not having many babies. They studied the problem for years. Finally, they discovered that DDT caused this problem. Today, DDT is not used in the United States. Safer poisons are used to kill insects. Eagles and other birds are laying normal eggs again.

Other substances move through a food chain the way DDT does. Some of these substances become problems for living things, including people.

Many scientists study the environment. When there is a problem, they try to find out

71

why. Then they look for ways to stop the problem.

Scientists have also helped find ways to reduce air and water pollution. New cars burn fuel better and produce fewer poisons. Factories, too, produce fewer poisons. There are laws against dumping poisons into rivers and lakes. People who break these laws can be arrested.

Problems with the health of the environment are still with us. But by knowing about them, we can do something. Humans can care for the environment so it will be a healthful place for all living things.

See also ecology.

epidemic, *see* disease and sickness

equator

The equator (ee-KWAY-tuhr) is an imaginary line around the earth halfway between the North Pole and the South Pole.

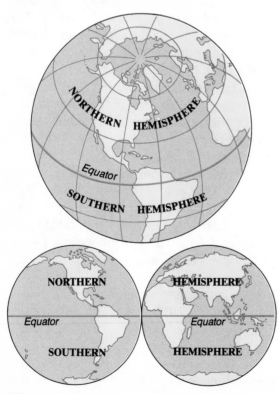

If you circled the globe along the equator, you would travel almost 25,000 miles (40,000 kilometers). More than three-fourths of your trip would be over ocean. One-fourth would be over land, through parts of South America, Africa, and some of the islands of Indonesia in Asia.

The equator divides the earth into two halves, called *hemispheres.* One difference between the hemispheres is that their seasons are reversed. In the Northern Hemisphere, summer begins in June, and winter begins in December. In the Southern Hemisphere, summer begins about December 21, and winter begins in June.

The equator helps us find places on maps and globes. Any place in the world can be located by its *latitude* and *longitude.* Latitude tells how far north or south of the equator a place is. The equator is 0° latitude. The North Pole is at 90° north latitude. Any point in the Northern Hemisphere is somewhere in between. Places in the Southern Hemisphere are located in degrees of south latitude. Any point in the Southern Hemisphere is somewhere between the equator and the South Pole.

See also latitude and longitude.

Equatorial Guinea, *see* Africa

Ericson, Leif

Leif Ericson (or Eriksson) was probably the first European to set foot on the North American mainland. He was called "Leif the Lucky" because of his sailing successes. His heroic deeds were recorded in long poems. These poems are called *sagas.*

Ericson was a Viking. The Vikings were people from northern Europe who began sailing to many different regions around the year 800. Leif's father was known as Eric the Red. He discovered Greenland. Leif was born in Iceland but was living in Greenland when he set sail on the voyage that led him to America. (*See* Vikings.)

Ericson and his crew reached America sometime around the year 1000. According to one saga, he landed in North America by accident. Another saga says he planned the expedition very carefully.

Ericson called the new land "Vinland" because he found wild grapevines growing there. Probably he landed in what is now Nova Scotia, or in New England.

Leif Ericson did not know that he had found a continent unknown to Europe. It was not recognized as a "new world" until Christopher Columbus made his famous voyage in 1492. But Ericson's achievement was a great one all the same.

Erie, Lake, *see* Great Lakes

Erie Canal

The Erie Canal is a man-made waterway that crosses the state of New York from Lake Erie to the Hudson River. It was built in the early 1800s to connect the East Coast with the rich lands around the Great Lakes.

President George Washington thought a canal was needed to tie the Eastern part of the country to the Midwest. Surveyors told him that building a canal through the long Mohawk Valley would be a huge job. So the idea was dropped.

In 1810, the mayor of New York City, De Witt Clinton, raised the idea again. At New York City, the Hudson River empties into the Atlantic. Clinton thought the canal would make his city the nation's leading port. Passengers and goods could come into New York City and travel up the Hudson River to Albany. From there, they could cross the state to Buffalo by canal, and move even farther west through Lake Erie.

In 1817, Clinton became governor of New York State. He was able to persuade the state legislature to provide the money—more than $7 million—to build the canal.

Many people laughed at his idea, calling it "Clinton's Ditch," but work began anyway. Thousands of workers began cutting down trees, clearing swamps, and blasting through rock along the route. It was 360-miles (581-kilometers) long. Following them came workers with picks, shovels, and mule-drawn bulldozers. The canal would be 40 feet (12 meters) wide and 4 feet (1.25 meters) deep.

Below, a map shows that the Erie Canal connects Lake Erie and the Atlantic Ocean. Barges carried crops from the Midwest to the East and goods from the East to the Midwest. Left, a section of the Erie Canal today.

Eight years later, on November 4, 1825, Governor Clinton stood on the deck of the *Seneca Chief* in New York Harbor and poured a bucket of Lake Erie water overboard. This "marriage of the waters" symbolized the joining of Lake Erie and the Atlantic.

Hundreds of flat boats called *barges* were towed back and forth along the canal by horses or mules walking slowly along the banks. Every now and then, a cry would ring out—"Low bridge, everybody down." Passengers quickly ducked.

The Erie Canal quickly paid for itself. It carried thousands of settlers to the rich lands westward. It carried factory goods to help pioneers set up farms. Crops were shipped eastward to feed people in eastern cities. So were furs from forests around the Great Lakes and the Mississippi River. New York City became the nation's busiest port.

The Erie Canal has since been enlarged several times. In 1918, it was combined with three shorter canals, forming the New York State Barge Canal System.

erosion

Erosion is nature's way of wearing down hills and cliffs and of carving valleys and canyons. To do this, nature uses several powerful tools—gravity, running water, ice, wind, and ocean waves.

Erosion due to running water begins with rain. Falling rain turns the soil muddy as the rainwater mixes with the soil. Gravity causes the water to flow downhill, and it picks up even more soil along the way.

Ice, temperature changes, and chemical changes cause the process called *weathering.* Over many years, weathering breaks rock on a hillside or mountain into small pieces. Then the force of gravity tugs the pieces downhill. After sliding or rolling down a hillside, the pieces may land in a stream. The running water sends them tumbling downstream. The pieces of rock are worn down as they tumble against each other

Water erosion washes away hillsides like this one and wears down whole mountains.

in the stream. When the rocks are worn down to the size of sand grains, they are called *sediment.* (*See* **weathering.**)

On coasts where there is no protective barrier island, ocean waves break directly against the cliffs. The waves tear away chunks of rock and roll them about in the surf. Eventually, they are broken into sand.

In dry desert areas, nature uses wind to carve rocks into fantastic shapes. Each grain of sand that the wind picks up becomes a tiny chisel. As the wind sweeps these tiny grains along, they cut and scratch any surface they meet.

Ice, too, is a powerful tool of erosion. Today, most erosion by ice occurs in mountainous areas that have large masses of ice called *glaciers.* Gravity pulls the glaciers slowly downhill. As they move, chunks of rock get stuck in the ice. Like a giant piece of sandpaper, the glacier grinds down the floor and walls of the valley. (*See* **glacier.**)

We can see the effects of erosion on land. But erosion also happens on the ocean floor. Fast-moving currents of water erode underwater rocks in the same way that rivers erode rock on land. Over a period of many years, the currents carve out canyons under

In Utah, wind erosion has helped carve rocks into strange and interesting shapes.

the water. Off the eastern coast of the United States, there are deep submarine canyons.

See also **canyon; conservation;** and **earth history.**

Eskimo

The Eskimo are a hardy people of the Far North. There are about 100,000 Eskimo. Their homeland is the frozen Arctic region. About half live in Greenland. Around 1,500 live in Siberia, in the Soviet Union. The rest live in Alaska and northern Canada.

Most Eskimo are rather short and stocky, with straight black hair. They are related to the people of eastern Asia. The ancestors of American and Greenland Eskimo probably came there from Siberia by boat about 10,000 years ago.

Today, most Eskimo live like the non-Eskimo people of the northlands. They fish or hunt for a living, or work in factories or on construction jobs. They live in wooden houses and travel by snowmobile. Until about 50 years ago, however, the Eskimo had a very different way of life.

Fishing and Hunting The land of the Eskimo is cold and harsh. It is covered by snow and ice six to nine months of the year. Crops cannot grow in the Arctic, and there are few trees. The Eskimo lived almost entirely on fish, whales, seals, and other animals they killed at sea and on land. They fished with bone hooks or spears. In winter, they fished through holes cut in the ice. Seals and whales were harpooned.

A man sometimes went seal-hunting by himself, in a *kayak*—an Eskimo canoe. Over his clothes, he wore a waterproof sealskin covering that fastened around the top of the kayak. If the boat turned over in rough seas, water could not get in, and he could easily turn it upright again. To hunt whales, several men would go out together in a bigger boat, an *umiak*. Both of these boats—the kayak and the umiak—were made of animal skins stretched tightly over ribs made of driftwood or bone.

The caribou was an important land animal for the Eskimo. Groups of men went out to hunt it with bows and arrows. Later, the Eskimo bought guns for caribou hunting.

The Eskimo had to move about in search of game. In winter, they traveled by dogsled. A dogsled was usually made of driftwood, with runners of wood or bone. It was hitched to as many dogs as an Eskimo family could afford to feed.

The Eskimo use small boats called *kayaks* for seal hunting.

In this Alaskan Eskimo game, people throw a person up in the air in a skin blanket.

The Eskimo used almost every part of the animals they hunted. They used bone for fishhooks, sewing needles, spears, tools, and boat frames. Skins and furs were turned into clothing, rugs, blankets, shoes, tents, and kayaks. Seal oil was burned in lamps.

Everyday Life In summer, the Eskimo usually lived in tents made of sealskin or caribou skin. In winter, many lived in small driftwood cabins or in stone huts. The roofs were made of whale ribs and sod—chunks of earth with moss or grass growing on it. The cabins had no windows. Instead, there were skylights made of animal tissue.

The best-known Eskimo winter house was the dome-shaped snow *igloo*. It was usually a temporary home, used only for a night or two on a hunting expedition. It could be built in an hour by cutting hardened snow into blocks and stacking them in a circle. Each layer of blocks was moved a little closer toward the center until the sides met at the top. Inside were snow platforms covered with furs. An igloo was warmed by lamps that burned animal fat. There might be a skylight made from a piece of clear ice.

Because fuel was so scarce, the Eskimo usually ate uncooked meat or fish. In fact, the Indian word *Eskimo* means "eater of raw meat." The Eskimo prefer to call themselves "Inuit," which means "the people."

The Eskimo made their clothes from the animals they killed for food. Everyone wore trousers, a hooded jacket, socks, boots, and mittens. The hooded jacket has been adopted by people all over the world. We still call it by its Eskimo name, *parka.*

In very cold weather, Eskimo wore two sets of clothing. They wore the inner set with the fur facing in and the outer set with the fur facing out. Warm air was trapped between the two layers.

Sun shining on snow can be painfully bright. So the Eskimo invented sun goggles. These were made from strips of bone or wood with small slits to look through.

Customs and Beliefs Sharing was basic to Eskimo life. No one owned land or water rights. If a family moved out of a house, anyone else could move in. When a hunter returned with food, everyone got some of it.

Eskimo families have always been warm and close-knit. The Eskimo love children and had as many as they could. A father would carve toys for his children to play with—dolls, animals, and tops made of ivory or wood.

Each family member, except for babies, had a job to do. A man's job was hunting. He began going along on hunting trips at age 12. A woman's main jobs were childcare and making clothing.

In spite of their harsh surroundings—or maybe because of them—the Eskimo have always been cheerful people who like company. They still enjoy getting together to re-tell old stories and sing old songs.

Estonia, *see* **Soviet Union**

Ethiopia

Capital: Addis Ababa
Area: 471,800 square miles (1,221,900 square kilometers)
Population (1985): about 42,266,000
Official language: Amharic

Ethiopia is a country in northeastern Africa. It faces the Red Sea and borders the countries of Djibouti, Somalia, Kenya, and the Sudan. Ethiopia has more land than Texas and California combined, and about the same number of people. In Africa, only Nigeria and Egypt have more people.

A mountainous plateau covers the western part of Ethiopia. The Blue Nile, which flows into the Nile River, begins in the mountains of this plateau. The Great Rift Valley cuts through the plateau, roughly from the Red Sea in the northeast to Lake Rudolph in the southwest.

Although Ethiopia is just north of the equator, the high plateau region has a cool climate. Yet the lowlands of Ethiopia are among the hottest places on earth.

Most Ethiopians live in villages in the cool mountains and work on small farms. They tend sheep, goats, and cattle and raise a variety of crops. They grow coffee for export. Ethiopia's capital and largest city, Addis Ababa, is in the mountains.

In the mountains of western Ethiopia, a boy tends his animals.

Ethiopia also has nomads. They do not grow crops, but are always traveling, looking for food. (*See* **nomad.**)

About half of the people of Ethiopia are Christian. This is unusual for an African nation. Most of the rest are Muslim. A group of Muslims from Somalia lives on the coast of the Red Sea. They have been fighting to make their land, Eritrea, part of Somalia.

Ethiopia has been independent longer than any other country in Africa. It was founded 3,000 years ago and was known as Abyssinia. Ethiopian legend says its kings and emperors can trace their line back to the Queen of Sheba. (*See* **African civilizations.**)

For most of the 1900s, Ethiopia was ruled by kings. King Menelik II, who ruled in the early 1900s, is considered the founder of modern Ethiopia. Haile Selassie I was Ethiopia's last emperor. He ruled until 1974, when the army overthrew him. The army still rules Ethiopia.

Today, Ethiopia is a very poor country. Ethiopia's soil is fertile, but it receives little rain. The country cannot grow enough food, and thousands of its people face starvation. Civil wars, disease, and famine have forced many to flee to neighboring countries.

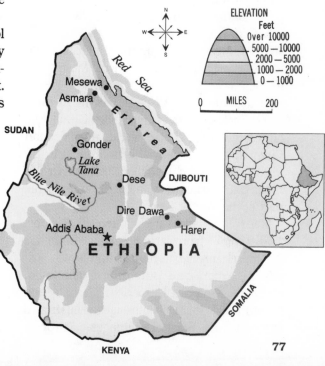

Europe

Europe is the continent directly east of the United States across the Atlantic Ocean. It is the second-smallest continent in the world—only Australia is smaller. But Europe has more people than any continent except Asia. Europe has about 700 million people—about three times as many as the United States. Many of the people of North, Central, and South America can trace their families back to a country in Europe.

In land area, Europe is slightly larger than the United States. From north to south, it is about 4,000 miles (6,400 kilometers) long. From east to west, it is about 3,000 miles (4,800 kilometers) wide.

Europe is surrounded on three sides by water. To its west is the Atlantic Ocean. To the north is the Arctic Ocean. To the south is the Mediterranean Sea, which separates Europe from Africa.

In the east, Europe is connected to the continent of Asia. We sometimes think of Europe and Asia as a single continent—Eurasia. One huge country, the Soviet Union, stretches from central Europe all the way across Asia to the Pacific Ocean. We usually think of the Soviet Union as a European country, even though most of its land is actually in Asia. Most maps show Europe stretching east as far as the Black Sea and the Caspian Sea, and to the Ural Mountains in the Soviet Union.

In all, there are 33 countries in Europe. These include part of the Soviet Union, the largest country in the world, and Vatican City, which is actually the smallest country in the world. A small part of Turkey is in Europe, but Turkey is usually thought of as part of the Middle East.

Many languages are spoken in Europe. They come from three major language groups: Germanic, Romance, and Slavic. English, German, and Dutch are examples of Germanic languages. Spanish, French, and Italian are Romance languages. Polish and Russian are Slavic languages. Europe's

Europe has beautiful mountains like those in Norway (right), handsome cities like Brugge, Belgium (below), and warm Mediterranean beaches like the one in Amalfi, Italy (below right).

many languages remind us that there was a time when Europe was made up of many tiny kingdoms.

Today, the countries of Europe are often thought of as Eastern European countries or Western European countries.

Western Europe The countries of Western Europe have democratic governments. Many Western European nations belong to the European Economic Community—the Common Market. The European Economic Community helps its member countries promote trade and protect their interests.

Western Europe is the part of the continent that faces the Atlantic Ocean. Warm currents in the Atlantic give much of Western Europe a fairly mild climate.

Western Europe is less than half the size of the United States. But it has about one and a half times the number of people. Western Europe is prosperous. It has fertile farmlands and rich mineral deposits. There is oil beneath the North Sea. The factories of

Western Europe produce a wide variety of goods. These goods can be transported easily on its rivers and canals.

At the northwest corner of Western Europe is the United Kingdom, made up of England, Scotland, Wales, and Northern Ireland. It is also called Great Britain, or Britain. Great Britain once ruled an empire that circled the world. Today, Britain is much less powerful but is still an important industrial country. (*See* **United Kingdom.**)

For a long time, Ireland was part of the British Empire. It became an independent country in 1949. In the mid-1800s, there were years of famine in Ireland. Many Irish people died or left the country. (*See* **Ireland.**)

In the past, France has ruled large areas of Europe. Today, it is the largest country in Western Europe. France has rich farmland and other natural resources. It is an important manufacturing country and a center of art and culture. (*See* **France.**)

In 1945, after World War II, Germany was divided into West Germany and East Germany. East Germany is part of Eastern Europe. West Germany is an industrial country that produces steel, iron, and chemicals. West German people have a high standard of living. (*See* **Germany.**)

Three small countries—Belgium, the Netherlands, and Luxembourg—are between France and West Germany. They are called the Low Countries because their land is not much above the level of the sea. Parts of the Netherlands are actually below sea level. (*See* **Netherlands, The.**)

COUNTRIES OF EUROPE

Country	Capital	Square Miles	Square Kilometers	Population
Albania	Tiranë	11,100	28,749	2,960,000
Andorra	Andorra la Vella	175	453	47,000
Austria	Vienna	32,374	83,848	7,548,000
Belgium	Brussels	11,781	30,512	9,858,000
Bulgaria	Sofia	42,823	110,911	8,974,000
Czechoslovakia	Prague	49,370	127,868	15,502,000
Denmark	Copenhagen	16,629	43,069	5,104,000
Finland	Helsinki	130,119	337,008	4,908,000
France	Paris	221,207	572,926	55,041,000
Germany (East)	Berlin	41,768	108,179	16,686,000
Germany (West)	Bonn	95,976	248,577	60,950,000
Great Britain	London	94,251	244,110	56,019,000
Greece	Athens	50,944	131,944	9,921,000
Hungary	Budapest	35,919	93,030	10,644,000
Iceland	Reykjavik	39,768	102,999	241,000
Ireland	Dublin	27,136	70,282	3,588,000
Italy	Rome	116,303	301,224	57,116,000
Liechtenstein	Vaduz	61	157	26,000
Luxembourg	Luxembourg	998	2,584	366,000
Monaco	Monaco-Ville	*	2	28,000
Netherlands	Amsterdam	15,770	40,844	14,481,000
Norway	Oslo	125,181	324,218	4,152,000
Poland	Warsaw	120,725	312,677	37,233,000
Portugal	Lisbon	35,553	92,082	10,046,000
Romania	Bucharest	91,699	237,500	22,734,000
San Marino	San Marino	24	62	23,000
Soviet Union	Moscow	8,649,496	22,402,194	277,504,000
Spain	Madrid	194,896	504,780	38,829,000
Sweden	Stockholm	173,731	449,963	8,348,000
Switzerland	Bern	15,941	41,287	6,457,000
Turkey	Ankara	301,381	780,576	50,661,000
Vatican City	—	*	*	1,000
Yugoslavia	Belgrade	98,766	255,803	23,124,000
TOTAL		10,841,865	28,080,418	819,120,000

*less than 1

Switzerland, Austria, and Liechtenstein lie south of Germany, in the Alps. These countries are *landlocked*—they have no outlet to the sea. Their people speak German. The people of Switzerland also speak French and Italian. Switzerland is a *neutral* country. It does not take sides or fight in wars. (*See* **Switzerland** and **Austria**.)

South of the Alps are the countries of Europe that border the Mediterranean Sea. Italy occupies a large peninsula shaped like a boot. The capital, Rome, was the center of the Roman Empire. Today, Italy is an important industrial country. (*See* **Italy**.)

East of Italy is Greece, a mountainous country with little farmland. Islands in the Mediterranean Sea make up part of Greece. (*See* **Greece** and **Greece, ancient**.)

Spain and Portugal are west of Italy on a peninsula that separates the Mediterranean Sea from the Atlantic. In the late 1400s, Spain and Portugal sent explorers west across the Atlantic and south around Africa. Each country had a large empire in the Americas and colonies in Asia and Africa. Today, Spain and Portugal are farming countries, producing olives, grapes, and wine. (*See* **Spain; Portugal;** and **explorers**.)

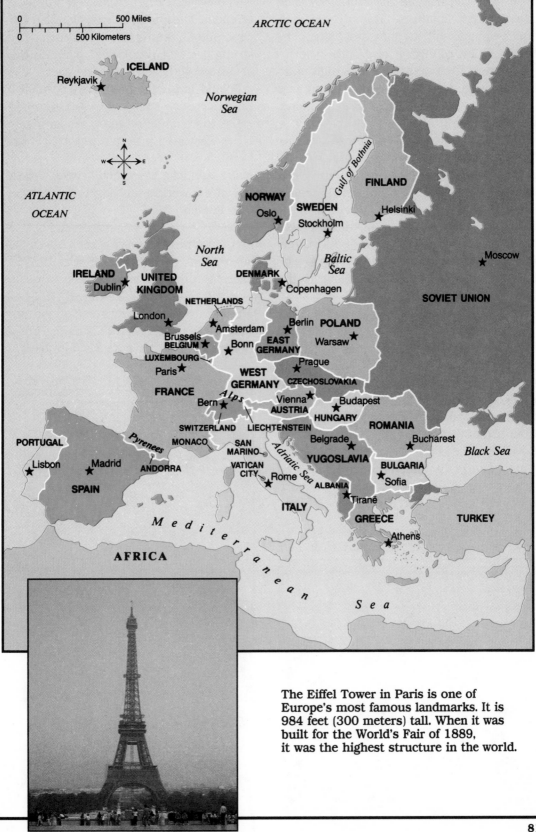

The Eiffel Tower in Paris is one of Europe's most famous landmarks. It is 984 feet (300 meters) tall. When it was built for the World's Fair of 1889, it was the highest structure in the world.

North of Germany is the Baltic Sea. The Scandinavian countries—Norway, Sweden, and Denmark—all jut into the Baltic. The Scandinavian countries have both factories and farms. Their people have a high standard of living. Iceland, an island nation, was colonized by Scandinavians. (*See* **Scandinavia** and **Iceland.**)

Finland is between Scandinavia and the Soviet Union. The Finnish language is related to Hungarian rather than to any Western European language. Finland's wealth comes from its thick forests.

Eastern Europe The countries of Eastern Europe cover an area about three-fourths the size of the United States. The Eastern European languages belong to the Slavic language group.

The Soviet Union has more land than any other country in the world. About one fourth of this land is in Eastern Europe, and about three fourths of the Soviet people live in Europe. There are more than 100 different ethnic groups in the country. The largest group are the Russian people, who make up more than half of the population. Until 1918, the Soviet Union was called "Russia." The Soviet Union has great mineral wealth, oil, and huge forests. Its farms produce a wide variety of crops. (*See* **Soviet Union.**)

This farmer in Romania lives and works much as his ancestors did centuries ago.

The Soviet Union has a communist government. The other countries in Eastern Europe have communist governments, and strong ties with the Soviet Union. But many also trade with nations of the West.

Poland is between the Soviet Union and East Germany. Except for the Soviet Union, it has more land and more people than any other Eastern European country. Poland's farmland is very fertile. Polish factories make steel, machines, and textiles. Poland is one of the world's largest producers of coal. (*See* **Poland.**)

East Germany, Poland's neighbor, has more factories than any other Eastern European country, except the Soviet Union. Its factories produce automobiles, iron, steel, plastics, and drugs. (*See* **Germany.**)

South of Poland and west of the Soviet Union are Czechoslovakia and Hungary. Both countries have fertile farmland and

These Austrian women are wearing traditional folk costumes and headdresses.

productive factories. Czechoslovakia is known for making high-quality machinery. Uranium is mined in Hungary. (*See* **Czechoslovakia** and **Hungary.**)

Yugoslavia is south of Hungary and across the Adriatic Sea from Italy. It has both farming and industry. The government owns most of the factories, but some are privately owned. (*See* **Yugoslavia.**)

Romania, Bulgaria, and Albania all border Yugoslavia. Romania and Bulgaria are to the east, between Yugoslavia and the Black Sea. Albania is located just south of Yugoslavia, and north of Greece. The rocky, mountainous land is poor farming country. But Romania is rich in oil.

History Ancient Greece is thought of as the birthplace of European civilization. Later, the Romans, who lived in Italy, controlled most of Europe. They spread Christianity and the Latin language. (*See* **Roman Empire.**)

The Roman Empire ended in the late 400s. The Dark Ages and Middle Ages followed. During this time, life was harsh. There were few developments in learning or the arts. Feudal lords ruled the countryside. During the Renaissance, which began in the 1300s, arts and sciences developed rapidly. European explorers introduced their languages and customs to many different parts of the world. (*See* **Dark Ages; Middle Ages;** and **Renaissance.**)

The Industrial Revolution, which began in the 1700s, changed the way people worked. Before the Industrial Revolution, most people worked on farms. Today, most live and work in cities. (*See* **Industrial Revolution.**)

The people of Europe have accomplished a great deal. But they have also suffered many wars. In this century alone, two world wars have done great damage in Europe.

See also **Crusades; World War I;** and **World War II.**

This beautifully decorated hall is a part of the palace at Versailles in France. Millions of people visit Europe each year to see its art and architecture.

When water evaporates, water molecules escape from the liquid into the air.

evaporation

Do you remember the nursery song about a little spider who was trying to go up a waterspout? The rain washed him out. But then, "Out came the sun and dried up all the rain. So the eensy-weensy spider went up the spout again." This is an example of evaporation. The heat energy of the sun caused the rainwater to dry up—evaporate.

Water is usually a liquid. But you have seen water become a solid when it turns to ice. And when a puddle dries up on a sunny day, you are seeing water become a gas.

What happens when water evaporates from a puddle? Water is made of many very tiny particles called *molecules*. The molecules are constantly moving around. When the sunlight hits the puddle, the water molecules near the puddle's surface take some of the sun's energy. These energized molecules move around faster and more excitedly than before. Eventually, they escape into the air. In the air, these freed molecules can travel farther apart. They are still molecules of water, but they are no longer bound into a puddle. They are molecules of water vapor. They have evaporated from the puddle.

Water will also evaporate when it is boiled in a pot on a stove. In fact, the pot must be watched very carefully, because all the water may boil away and the pot will be damaged. Adding heat speeds up the rate of evaporation. The steam rising from the pot is molecules of water that have become molecules of water vapor—a gas.

Of course, water is not the only liquid that can evaporate. If you put rubbing alcohol on your skin, it will disappear even faster than water. That is because molecules of alcohol do not need much heat energy to go from a liquid to a gas. Your skin will feel cold where the alcohol was. The liquid alcohol molecules use the heat energy of your skin to change into gas molecules. In hot, dry places, where evaporation is rapid, people use evaporation to cool their homes.

See also **heat; gas; liquid; matter; molecule;** and **water cycle.**

Everest, Mount

Mount Everest is the highest mountain in the world. The peak rises 29,028 feet (8,848 meters) above sea level. This is 5½ miles (almost 9 kilometers)! Mount Everest is on the border of Nepal and Tibet, in southern Asia. It is in the Himalayas, the world's highest mountain range. Mount Everest was named for Sir George Everest, an Englishman. He established its location and estimated its height. (*See* **Himalayas.**)

Mount Everest is covered with snow all year round, except at the very top where fierce winds blow it away. Some of the winds blow at speeds of 200 miles (320 kilometers) per hour. Glaciers make their way down the sides of the mountain. Often, there are avalanches. (*See* **avalanche.**)

Very few plants or animals can live high up on Mount Everest. At that height, the air contains little oxygen for animals to breathe. Above 16,000 feet (4,900 meters) on the mountain, temperatures are below freezing, and it is almost always snowy.

Avalanches, thin air, and harsh weather make it very difficult to climb Everest. People began trying to climb the mountain in the 1920s. No one reached the top until 1953. Edmund Hillary and Tenzing Norgay were the first people to stand on the highest spot in the world. Edmund Hillary was from New Zealand. Tenzing Norgay was a Sherpa guide from Nepal. Their climb took 81 days.

Mount Everest, on the border of Nepal and Tibet, is the tallest of the many towering peaks in the Himalayas.

Since then, other people have successfully climbed Mount Everest. One Sherpa guide, Nawang Gombu, has reached the summit twice. In 1975, Junko Tabei of Japan became the first woman to reach the top of Mount Everest.

See also **mountain climbing.**

Everglades

The Everglades is a huge area of swamp and marshland in southern Florida. It covers over 2,700 square miles (7,000 square kilometers). This subtropical wilderness is the home of alligators, crocodiles, and many water birds.

The northern and eastern parts of the Everglades are covered with saw grass. There is so much saw grass that the Everglades is often called the "River of Grass."

Lake Okeechobee, one of the largest lakes in the United States, is at the northern end of the Everglades. Its name is an Indian word that means "big water."

During the rainy season, water flows out of Lake Okeechobee and through the Everglades. The swamp becomes a wide, shallow, slow-moving river that empties into the Gulf of Mexico.

In some areas, small hills called *hummocks* rise above the wet, swampy ground. Stands of cypress, mahogany, and pine trees grow on the hummocks, making them look like small islands of trees.

Tall cypress trees hung with Spanish moss grow in the Florida Everglades. This swamp in southern Florida is one of the largest in the world.

Two areas of the Everglades have been made into parks. Everglades National Park is in the south. It includes an area along Florida's west coast, on the Gulf of Mexico, called the Ten Thousand Islands. Big Cypress National Preserve is northwest of the national park. The Big Cypress preserve is covered with dense tropical rain forest.

These areas have colorful orchids as well as cypress, palm, and mangrove trees. Crocodiles and alligators slither through the swamps. Many kinds of snakes and giant turtles also live there. Wading birds—such as egrets, ibis, blue herons, and the spectacular great white heron—are a common sight.

The best way to travel through the Everglades is by airboat, but it is easy to get lost among the saw grass and "tree islands." Miccosukee Indians sometimes act as guides for visitors. Seminole and Miccosukee Indians once lived and hunted in the Everglades. Today, hunting is forbidden in Everglades National Park. Deer, hogs, and turkeys may be hunted in the Big Cypress preserve. Some Miccosukee still live in the Everglades, but not in Everglades National Park itself.

evergreen tree

Some trees keep their leaves all year long. These trees are called evergreen trees, or just evergreens. It is easy to see how they got their name. Christmas trees are usually evergreens. So is holly, which is often used in wreaths. Evergreen trees are found almost everywhere in the world.

Kinds of Evergreens Most of the trees in northern forests are evergreens. Many of these trees, such as spruces, firs, and pines, have leaves that are like needles. Other evergreen trees, such as junipers, have leaves like scales. All these evergreens can live in places without a lot of water. Their small leaves help the trees save water.

Northern evergreens live where there is a lot of snow. They are shaped like tepees— wide at the bottom and pointed at the top.

Their branches bend easily. When snow builds up on the branches, they bend and drop the snow. This keeps them from breaking under the snow's weight.

Some evergreen trees grow well in sandy soil. Sandy soil does not hold water very well. But pine trees can grow in this soil, because their needles keep them from losing water.

Junipers may grow in desert areas. In the desert, a juniper's trunk grows along the ground and its branches grow into the air. They get very little water, so they stay small.

Evergreen trees are green all year long, but this does not mean that they have just one set of leaves. They lose only a few of their leaves at a time. New leaves grow back as old leaves drop. You can tell this is true by looking under an evergreen tree. Dropped leaves form a carpet under the tree. The carpet under an old tree may be very deep.

Evergreen trees with needlelike and scalelike leaves are cone-bearing plants. These trees have two kinds of cones. One kind, the pollen cones, make pollen. The other kind, seed cones, are where the seeds grow. In the spring, pollen is released by the pollen cones. The pollen is carried through the air to the seed cones. The cones you think of as "pinecones" are the seed cones. (*See* cone-bearing plant.)

Evergreens come in many sizes (right), from the bushy rhododendron to the giant sequoia. Many have cones (below).

Broadleaf Evergreens Some evergreen trees are flowering plants. They make their seeds in flowers rather than in cones, and have large, wide leaves instead of needles.

Holly, mountain laurels, azaleas, and rhododendrons are broadleaf evergreens. There are male holly trees and female holly trees. The berries of the holly contain the seeds and are only on the female holly tree. Rhododendrons are large plants with pretty flowers and large, leathery leaves. Mountain laurel, a relative of the rhododendron, has smaller leaves and showy flowers. Azaleas have even smaller leaves. Azalea and rhododendron flowers are trumpet-shaped.

Most other broadleaf evergreens grow where it is warm and wet. They may grow very tall. Small plants often grow on the trunks of these evergreens.

The strangler fig is a broadleaf evergreen that kills other trees. Its seeds sprout when they fall onto a branch of another tree. As the roots grow to the ground, they wrap around the trunk of the tree. The roots grow thicker and soon kill the host tree.

sequoia

fir

blue spruce

white pine

orange

rhododendron

This redwood is the world's tallest tree—
about the height of a 30-story building.

Evergreens Are Record-Holders Evergreen trees are among the tallest and the oldest living things on earth. California's coastal redwoods are the tallest. The tallest coastal redwood is 112 meters (366 feet) high. The second-tallest living things are also evergreens. They are the tapangs of tropical forests in Asia. These broadleaf evergreens grow to be 48 to 80 meters (150 to 250 feet) tall. (*See* **redwoods and sequoias**.)

The oldest living trees are bristlecone pines, which grow in the southwestern part of the United States. Some bristlecone pines growing in the White Mountains along the border of California and Nevada are more than 4,600 years old.

Many living things make their homes in evergreen forests. Birds nest on branches.

Insects live under bark. In tropical forests, monkeys and other animals live in evergreens. The trees' berries and seeds provide food.

Uses of Evergreen Trees Evergreen trees give us many important things. The trunks of pine and fir trees are made into lumber. Evergreen trees also supply the wood pulp used to make paper and cardboard. Turpentine comes from the sap of some kinds of evergreens. It is used to clean paintbrushes and to thin paint.

Broadleaf evergreens, too, give us important products. Cinnamon, a favorite spice, is the crushed bark of a small evergreen tree. Camphor, a strong-smelling oil from evergreens, is used in perfumes and cold medicines. Trees that produce natural rubber are also evergreen.

The fruits of some broadleaf evergreens are food for humans. Avocados grow on an evergreen tree. Citrus trees, including oranges, lemons, limes, grapefruits, and tangerines, are evergreens, too. These evergreens grow in warm areas of the United States, such as Florida and California.

Many people plant evergreens in their yards. Where winters are cold, evergreens look especially pretty when other trees have lost all their leaves. Evergreens can also be used as protection against bad weather. A row of evergreen trees blocks the winter wind and helps to keep a house warmer. They can block blowing snow, too. Evergreens also provide winter homes for birds. Chickadees, titmice, cardinals, and other birds will roost in evergreens during the winter.

Evert, Chris

Chris Evert, an American tennis champion, is considered to be one of the top women tennis players of all time. She started playing in tennis tournaments in 1970, when she was 16 years old. Since 1974, she has won about 1,200 tennis matches and 150 tournaments. This is more than any other player since tennis became a professional sport in 1968.

Christine Evert was born in Florida in 1954. Her father, a tennis instructor, began teaching her to play tennis when she was only six. She was not very strong, so she used both hands to hit a backhand shot. Later, her two-handed backhand became one of the most successful shots in tennis.

Chris Evert was ranked number one in the world for five years in a row, from 1974 to 1978. She played her best on clay tennis courts, and won 125 matches on clay in a row.

Evert regularly won the most important tennis tournaments, including the United States Open and Britain's Wimbledon. She also was the first woman to earn more than $1 million as an athlete. In the early 1980s, Chris Evert was challenged by Martina Navratilova. Martina became the new champion for the 1980s. Often, Chris and Martina faced each other in the finals of important tournaments.

Chris Evert was one of the most successful and admired tennis players in history.

evolution

Living things change over time. Some kinds of living things die out. Other kinds of living things take their places. This process of gradual change is called *evolution.*

Have you ever seen the skeleton of a dinosaur? These animals lived on earth a long time ago. Today, there are no living dinosaurs. When all the living things of one kind have died out, the living thing is *extinct.* Scientists believe that all dinosaurs became extinct millions of years ago. (*See* **dinosaur.**)

The skeleton of a dinosaur is a kind of *fossil.* There are many kinds of fossils. Footprints hardened into stone are fossils. The print of a leaf in sandstone is also a fossil. Fossils are evidence of living things of the past. Scientists study fossils to put together a picture of the past and understand how life on earth has changed. (*See* **fossil.**)

The fossil picture shows that a billion years ago, there were only tiny, one-celled living things. Later, there were thousands of kinds of living things in oceans that covered the earth. Still later, plants and animals living on land appear in the fossil record.

How Living Things Become Extinct Scientists study the changes they see in the fossil record. They use what they know about living things today to develop ideas about the past. Most scientists believe that the climate of the earth has changed several times. Each time the climate changed, many living things died out. Others have taken their place. The dinosaurs are a good example of this change. The plants the dinosaurs used for food could grow only in a warm, damp climate. Some scientists believe that as the climate became cooler, many plants died. The dinosaurs had no food, so they died, too.

Some scientists think the climate changed very quickly. They think a comet or asteroid struck the earth, and that the collision sent dust high in the atmosphere. It may also have set fire to forests, filling the air with more smoke and soot. The soot in the upper

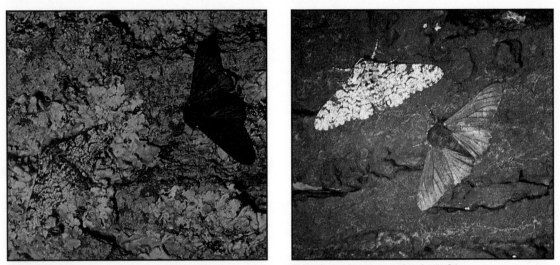

Peppered moths are gray so that they are camouflaged against gray bark (left).
But near big cities in England, soot made surfaces darker. Gray moths weren't as well
hidden (right). Darker peppered moths reproduced, producing a new black variety.

atmosphere would have blocked the sunlight. Without sunlight, Earth's surface would soon have become too cold for some plants and animals.

The last big climate change ended about 11,000 years ago. Until then, glaciers covered many parts of the earth. We call this period of earth's history the *Ice Age*. Before the time of the Ice Age, mammoths, mastodons, saber-toothed cats, and giant armadillos lived on earth. By the end of the Ice Age, these animals had died out. No one is sure why so many large animals became extinct when many smaller animals survived. Some scientists think that people learned to hunt some of the large animals, such as mammoths. People may have killed so many that eventually none were left. Other large mammals, such as the saber-toothed cats, may have become extinct because their prey was gone. (*See* **ice age** and **animals, prehistoric**.)

Causes of Evolution Charles Darwin is called the "father of evolution." He described how evolution works in nature. Darwin studied fossils and observed living things. He noticed that living things seemed to be designed for the way they lived. The beaks of seed-eating birds were suited for picking up and opening seeds. The beaks of meat-eating birds were specially suited for tearing their

prey. Swimming birds had webbed feet. Burrowing animals had feet suited to digging. Darwin decided that nature selects the living things that can survive best. It does this by causing weak and poorly suited living things to die out. The better-suited ones live to pass their traits on to their offspring. (*See* **Darwin, Charles**.)

Evolution may take millions of years. For this reason, it is hard for us to see evolution happening. But we have seen some examples. For awhile, a poison called DDT was

---

DDT and Evolution

When DDT is first used in a region, it kills nearly all houseflies. But after a few years, most flies are *resistant* to DDT — it does not kill them. The table below shows this change. At first, only a very few flies are resistant. They survive and reproduce. Their offspring are more likely to be resistant. After several generations, nearly all houseflies in a region become resistant.

Generation	Flies Sprayed	Flies Died	Flies Resistant To DDT
1	100	98	2
2	100	96	4
3	100	92	8
4	100	84	16
5	100	68	32
6	100	36	64
7	100	none	100

used to kill houseflies. But a few flies survived when they were sprayed with DDT. They lived to have many offspring. Each generation of their offspring produced more flies resistant to the poison.

Humans affect evolution in other ways. When we change the environment, we may take away the food or shelter of some living things. The ones that can switch to other kinds of food and shelter will survive and produce offspring adapted to the new environment. The ones that can't adjust to the new conditions will die out.

People are looking for ways to protect living things that are in danger of dying out. One way we do this is by protecting areas such as marshes where many plants and animals live. By these actions, we are trying to find ways to live with other living things.

See also **animals, endangered; birds of the past; mammals of the past; earth history;** and **environment.**

---

exercise, *see* aerobic exercise

---

experiment

To learn about the universe, scientists ask questions. One way a scientist finds the answers to questions is to do experiments. An experiment is a way to test an idea, to tell whether it is true or not. Some experiments are done just to find out what happens. The "father of modern science," Galileo, was the first scientist to use experiments as a way of answering questions. (*See* **Galileo.**)

You may not know it, but you do experiments, too. Have you ever given your pet a new food to see if your pet would eat it? Have you ever put a balloon in a refrigerator to see what would happen to the balloon? These are simple experiments.

Suppose you want to know if grass will grow in red light. To find out, plant grass seed in a flowerpot and put the pot where it will get only red light. If the pot gets any other light, it will spoil your experiment.

Does plant food make plants grow faster? An experiment with two plants—one that gets no plant food and one that does— will provide an answer.

Check the pot each day to be sure the soil is moist. Write down what you see. This is a record of the experiment.

If the grass grows, you know that grass can grow in red light. But you do not know if grass can grow in other colors of light, or if other plants can grow in red light. If no grass comes up, you may decide that grass cannot grow in red light. But you may wonder if you did something wrong or if something was wrong with the seed. You may want to try the experiment again.

Suppose you then want to know if a plant food will make grass grow faster. Plant seed from the same bag in two pots. Keep the two pots at the same temperature and give them the same amount of light and water. But feed plant food to just one of them. That one is called the *experimental plant.* The plant that does not get plant food is called the *control.* If the plant that gets plant food grows faster, you will know the plant food made it happen. Everything else was the same.

Some experiments require complex tools, such as microscopes and laser beams. Not all good experiments require complex tools. What any good experiment needs most are a good question and a clever experimenter.

Roald Amundsen's party (left) was the first to reach the South Pole in 1911. In modern times, Jacques Cousteau (right) was an explorer of the unknown world under the sea.

explorers

Explorers are people who travel far and wide in search of the unknown. They face many hardships—bad weather, dangerous conditions, and illness. Some explorers seek adventure. Others hope to find valuable raw materials, such as precious metals. Today's explorers often seek scientific information.

In the past, an explorer's home country often set up a *colony*—an overseas settlement—in the land he explored. Colonies are rare today. Most former colonies are now independent countries. (*See* **colony.**)

Many long-ago explorers left no written records, so we do not know who they were. For example, we do not know who the first people to travel from Asia to America were—the ancestors of the American Indians. In fact, most wonders of the world, such as great waterfalls and mountain ranges, were discovered by unknown adventurers. As you read about famous explorers, remember that most of them were following other brave people who left no records.

Early Explorers One of the first explorers we know about was a man named Hanno. He came from Carthage, on the Mediterranean Sea in what is now Tunisia. About 500 B.C.—some 2,500 years ago—Hanno made at least one voyage along the west coast of Africa. He wrote about seeing "little dark hairy people." These were not people at all, but apes.

Another explorer of ancient times was a Greek named Pytheas. About 200 years after Hanno, he sailed out of the Mediterranean Sea and headed north along the Atlantic coast of Europe. Pytheas was one of the first people to realize that the moon makes ocean water rise and fall, causing high and low tides.

Another Greek explorer, Hippalus, was one of many traders who traveled between Egypt and India. They made the trip by sailing close to the shores of Arabia and Pakistan. But Hippalus discovered a faster way. Ships could sail directly across the Indian Ocean with the help of certain winds.

Other brave traders developed the "Silk Route." This was a trail across Asia that linked the Mediterranean world with China. Europeans loved the beautiful silk fabrics made by the Chinese. Both Europeans and Chinese endured many hardships to buy and sell silk.

One of the greatest early travelers was a Chinese pilgrim named Hsuan-tsang. In the 600s, he crossed the great Gobi Desert alone. He then crossed the Hindu Kush Mountains of Afghanistan into India. There, he spent years visiting places sacred to Buddha. He finally returned home by way of Indochina.

Other Great Travelers In the years between 700 and 1200, there was little exploration. In Europe, this was a time called the Dark Ages, when people were poor and backward. The Chinese were more advanced, but wanted nothing to do with the outside world. The Vikings of northern Europe did voyage far from their homeland, but few people knew about it. (*See* **Dark Ages** and **Vikings**.)

In the early 1200s, the Mongols took over China and much of Asia. They welcomed outsiders. One traveler, an Italian named Marco Polo, not only visited the Mongol ruler of China but traveled to other places in Asia.

The greatest traveler of this period was an Arab, Ibn Battutah. Starting in 1325, he spent 30 years going from place to place. He went to Mecca, in Arabia, and then east to India, China, and many islands of Asia. He also journeyed to Spain and to the great African city of Timbuktu.

The Age of Exploration In the early 1400s, Europeans seemed to "wake up." Suddenly, they were full of energy. They began a great Age of Exploration, inspired mainly by a Portuguese prince, Henry the Navigator. He set up a center where sailors and sea captains could exchange information. He encouraged men to explore the unknown. From then on, explorers tried to build on each other's work instead of finding things by chance. Their knowledge was spread by printed books, developed in the late 1400s. (*See* **printing**.)

The seamen of the Age of Exploration were aided by several things that made sailing easier and safer. One was a new kind of ship, the *caravel*. It could sail faster and travel longer away from land. Better charts and maps helped seamen find out where they were. So did the compass. (*See* **compass**.)

Under Prince Henry's direction, ships sailed farther and farther south along the coast of Africa. In 1488, Bartolomeu Dias reached the Cape of Good Hope. A few years later, Vasco da Gama went around the tip of Africa and all the way to India.

In 1492, Christopher Columbus made his famous voyage to America, claiming it for Spain. Colonies and further exploration followed. Spanish adventurers included Vasco Núñez de Balboa, Francisco Coronado, Hernando Cortés, and Francisco Pizarro. France sent men like Jacques Cartier and Samuel de Champlain. John Cabot and Sir Francis Drake explored for England.

Probably the most daring voyage during the Age of Exploration was that of Ferdinand Magellan. He proved that people could sail around the world, but he died along the way. By 1700, Europeans had crossed most of the great seas and explored thousands of miles of coastlines.

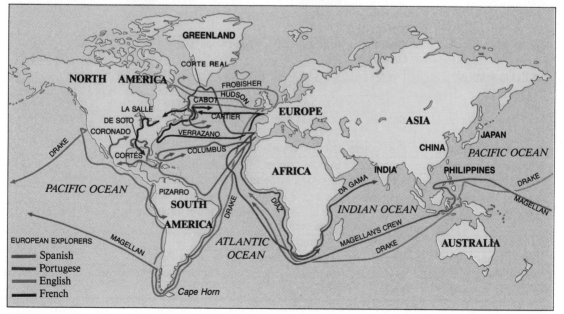

More Recent Exploration In the years after the Age of Exploration, James Cook explored Hawaii, Australia, and New Zealand. David Livingstone and Henry Stanley spent years in Africa. Explorers of the 1900s have been helped by inventions such as radio, radar, and airplanes. Even so, exploration still requires nerve and skill.

The icy North Pole and South Pole have attracted many explorers. Among them were Roald Amundsen, Robert Peary, and Robert Scott. Modern-day explorers have walked on the ocean floor—and found remains of ships sailed by earlier explorers. Since the 1950s, astronauts have ventured many thousands of miles into space. (*See* **space exploration.**)

No one knows what future explorers will find. But it seems certain that as long as there is an unknown, people will want to learn more about it.

FAMOUS EXPLORERS

Name	Nationality	Accomplishment	Year
*Amundsen, Roald	Norwegian	first to reach South Pole	1911
Armstrong, Neil	American	first person to set foot on moon	1969
*Balboa, Vasco Núñez de	Spanish	first European to see Pacific Ocean from eastern coast	1513
*Boone, Daniel	American	explored western frontier of United States	late 1700s
*Cabot, John	Italian	first European to explore eastern Canada	1497
*Cartier, Jacques	French	explored Gulf of St. Lawrence and St. Lawrence River	1534-42
Champlain, Samuel de	French	explored Great Lakes region and Lake Champlain	1603-15
*Columbus, Christopher	Italian	made America known to Europe	1492
Cook, James	English	explored South Pacific	1770s
Coronado, Francisco	Spanish	explored western North America	1540-42
*Cortés, Hernando	Spanish	led first Europeans through Aztec empire (Mexico)	1519-21
*Da Gama, Vasco	Portuguese	first European to reach India by sea	1498
*De Soto, Hernando	Spanish	first European to see Mississippi River	1540
*Drake, Sir Francis	English	explored California; sailed around world	1577-80
*Ericson, Leif	Norse	probably first European to voyage to America	1000
*Hudson, Henry	English	explored Hudson Bay and Hudson River	1609-11
Ibn Battūtah	Arab from Morocco	traveled throughout North Africa and Asia	1325-52
*Jolliet, Louis	French-Canadian	explored upper Mississippi River	1673
*La Salle, Sieur de	French	first European to sail down Mississippi River to Gulf of Mexico	1682
*Lewis and Clark	American	explored far western United States	1804-06
Livingstone, David	Scottish	explored southern Africa; first European to see Victoria Falls	1840s-1871
*Magellan, Ferdinand	Portuguese	led first voyage to sail around world	1519-22
*Marquette, Jacques	French	explored upper Mississippi River	1673
*Peary, Robert E.	American	first explorer to reach North Pole	1909
*Pizarro, Francisco	Spanish	led first Europeans through Inca empire (Peru)	1532
*Polo, Marco	Italian	one of first Europeans to travel through much of eastern Asia	late 1200s
*Ponce de León	Spanish	explored Florida	1513
*Scott, Robert	English	led second expedition to South Pole	1912
Thompson, David	Canadian	explored Pacific Northwest and Columbia River	1790s-early 1800s
*Vespucci, Amerigo	Italian	explored South America	early 1500s

Explorers with a * before their name have an entry in the *Golden Book Encyclopedia*.

Explosives can tear down an old building in a few seconds. The explosives are carefully set so that the building will fall in upon itself.

explosive

A material that takes up a small space but can produce violently expanding gases is an explosive. Explosives cause sparkling fireworks to flame across the sky. They propel the bullets from a hunter's gun. They can also topple old buildings to make room for new ones. Explosives can even blast tunnels through mountains.

Usually heat, a spark, or a shock starts the explosion. For example, a bullet has a small cap called a *detonator*. The detonator has a tiny amount of an explosive. When you pull the trigger of the gun, a hammer hits the detonator. The small explosion of the detonator lights a larger amount of gunpowder and starts a larger explosion. The rapidly expanding gases send the bullet speeding out of the barrel.

The explosions that propel a bullet or drive a rocket are controlled. We call controlled explosives *propellants*.

The powerful explosives used for blasting rocks are called *high explosives*. They can develop temperatures as high as 5,000° C (9000° F). TNT is the most widely used high explosive. Other important high explosives are dynamite and RDX.

When traveling, you may have seen a sign along the road saying "Turn off two-way radios. Explosives being used." People whose job is to set off the explosives do not want to be too close when they explode. They move a safe distance away. Then they signal the explosives with a radio. When a small radio receiver gets the signal, it produces a spark that ignites the explosive. Your two-way radio could cause the explosion to happen too soon.

High explosives are used to level the land before building highways, to tunnel through mountains, and to dig out mines. It would be difficult to imagine modern life without these useful explosives. But these same explosives can be used to make bombs that can cause terrible damage.

All explosives are dangerous! You should stay far away from where they are being used. It is especially dangerous to strike bullets with a rock or hammer or to throw them into the fire. Experienced professionals are hired to set off the fireworks we enjoy on the Fourth of July.

eye

The eye is our most important way of finding out about the world around us. We use our eyes for reading, working, and playing. One of the few times we do not use our eyes is when we are sleeping!

Your eyes are well protected. Each eye is set in a cone-shaped hole in the skull called the *eye socket.* The *eyelids* serve as a protective cover over your eyes. *Eyelashes* catch dust and dirt that might otherwise enter your eyes. Tears from tear glands wash away dirt that gets into your eyes.

The outside layer of your eyeball is made of tough tissues. The colored part of your eye, the *iris,* is covered by a transparent—clear—material called the *cornea.* The inside of the eye is filled with a jellylike substance that helps the eyeball keep its shape.

The eye works like a camera. A camera has an opening to let in light. The eye, too, has an opening, called the *pupil.* The pupil looks like a black dot at the center of your eye, but it is really a hole. The iris contains muscles that control the size of the pupil. In dim light, the pupil gets larger to let in more light. In bright light, the pupil gets smaller.

Both a camera and an eye contain a lens. In a camera, the lens forms a picture on the film. In an eye, the lens forms a picture on the back wall of the eye. This back wall is

A fly has giant compound eyes, each made of thousands of separate sensors.

called the *retina.* Muscles in the eye adjust the shape of the lens about 100,000 times a day to keep the picture sharp.

Camera film contains chemicals that respond to light. The retina contains two kinds of light-sensitive cells. The *rod cells* respond in very dim light. The *cone cells* react to very bright light. The cone cells also sense colors. Rods and cones are attached to nerve cells that send information to the brain in the form of nerve impulses.

Many adult insects have both *simple eyes* and *compound eyes.* A compound eye may have thousands of lenses! Each lens sees just a small piece of the whole picture.

Not all animals can see colors. Some fish, birds, and bees see the colors we see. But cats have very little color vision, and dogs probably none at all. Apes are among the few mammals that see color the way humans do.

See also **sight.**

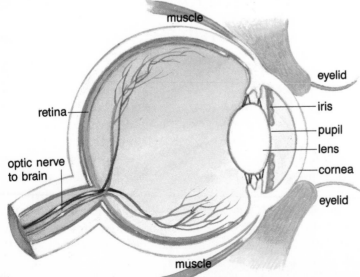

muscle

retina

optic nerve to brain

eyelid

iris

pupil

lens

cornea

eyelid

muscle

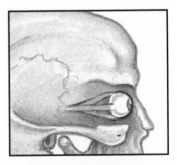

Light enters the human eye through the pupil and forms an image on the retina. Nerves carry information to the brain.